VICTORIAN
MANCHESTER AND SALFORD

Titles of related interest from Ryburn Publishing:

Victorian Bradford   The Living Past
Photographs by Ian Beesley   Commentary by David James

The Ryburn Map of Victorian Bradford
Text by Elvira Willmott

Calderdale: Architecture and History
Photographs by Ian Beesley and Andrew Caveney
Commentary by Alan Betteridge, Derek Bridge and Peter H. Thornborrow

Forthcoming:

Warwickshire Hatters
Photographs by Ian Beesley   Commentary by Judy Vero

Town and City Histories: A History of Bradford
by David James   Photographs by Andrew Caveney

The Living Past Series

VICTORIAN MANCHESTER AND SALFORD

Photographs by

IAN BEESLEY

Introduction and Commentary by

PETER DE FIGUEIREDO

Ryburn Publishing

First published in 1988
by Ryburn Publishing Ltd
Krumlin, Halifax, England

Artwork and typesetting by
Armitage Typo/Graphics, Huddersfield
Printed and bound by
The Amadeus Press, Huddersfield

The Living Past Series
ISSN 0954-1934
Victorian Manchester and Salford
ISBN 1-85331-006-9

Introduction

"Certainly Manchester is the most wonderful city of modern times." Thus was the hero of Disraeli's novel 'Coningsby', published in 1844, urged to visit this "Lancashire village... expanded into a mighty region of factories and warehouses," and he hurried to see it. So too did a host of 19th century writers and travellers; they went away both fascinated and appalled.

It was the seamier side of life to which many drew attention. Disraeli himself visited Manchester and in another of his novels, 'Sibyl' or 'The Two Nations', he described the wretched living conditions of the factory workers. Most graphic was the account given by the Frenchman Alexis de Tocqueville who journeyed through England in 1835. "On ground below the level of the river and overshadowed on all sides by immense workshops spreads a marshy land in which widely spaced, muddy ditches can neither drain nor cleanse − narrow twisting roads lead down to it. These lanes are lined with one storey houses whose ill-fitting planks and broken windows show them up − even from a long distance − as the final refuge for a man torn betweeen poverty and death." Even these miserable dwellings, de Tocqueville claimed, were the envy of some inhabitants, for they lived in the notorious cellars which represented some of the most appalling living conditions in Britain.

In the 1840s Manchester was a city of unfettered capitalism: "On this waterlogged landscape," observed de Tocqueville, "which both nature and art have contributed to keep damp, are scattered palaces and hovels. Everything about the exterior appearance of the city attests to man's individual power; nothing to the directing power of society." Like the great mercantile cities of the middle ages − Florence or Bruges − Manchester was dominated by ambitious and ruthless entrepreneurs. Wages were kept low by the arrival of large numbers of Irish immigrants, labour relations were bad, and disease amongst the poorest inhabitants was rife. But as a Manchester 'middle class gentleman' told Friedrich Engels after listening to a diatribe about the conditions of the workers, "And yet there is a great deal of money made here. Good morning, sir."

Cotton was the source of this wealth and Manchester was 'Cottonopolis'. The city was well placed to capitalise on developments in textile manufacture. It was close to Liverpool, the natural port for American cotton, and enjoyed a damp climate and plentiful fresh water. The introduction of steam power and factory production slashed the cost of cotton goods. In 1786 cotton yarn sold in Manchester for 38/- per pound; in 1833 it was 2/11d. The whole world wanted cotton and suddenly could afford it. The erection of mills, warehouses and dwellings could scarcely keep up with demand, and the population grew from 40,000 in 1774 to 280,000 in 1831 and over 600,000 in 1900. This rapid industrialisation posed frightening problems of social and political control, with the result that Manchester became a major new force in British politics. There was the issue of Law and Order, highlighted by the scandal of the Peterloo Massacre of 1819 when troops were used to quash a radical meeting; of Free Trade, which the city promoted; of Reform, for Manchester was denied a parliamentary voice until 1832; of Education, represented by the opening in Salford of the first Free Library in 1852; of the Press, for *The Manchester Guardian* was the voice of liberal independence; and of Labour, the cause of the Trades Union Congress which held its first meeting in Manchester in 1868. Amongst reformers the city can claim Engels and Dr James P. Kay, writers on working class conditions; Edwin Chadwick, public health campaigner; Robert Owen, socialist utopian; and Elizabeth Gaskell, author of novels on Manchester life.

Manchester was an exciting place. In her book 'North and South', Mrs Gaskell described the people of those times: "their energy, their power, their indomitable courage in struggling and fighting, their lurid vividness of existence," people always in a hurry, a vast force of human industry; whilst all around them "the chimneys smoked, the ceaseless roar and mighty beat and dazzling whirl of machinery struggled and strove perpetually."

As the century progressed, the role of Manchester changed from being a manufacturing town to a centre of trade and distribution, a change made possible by rapid improvements in transport. The Bridgewater Canal had opened in 1761 to carry coal into Manchester, and already by 1804 the town was linked by river and canal to a national water transport network. In 1830 the first passenger railway station was opened at Liverpool Road and this was followed by three more major termini, each with its own goods handling facilities and warehousing. In 1894 the Ship Canal brought ocean-going vessels right into Salford. Thus Manchester became the Mecca for traders and entrepreneurs connected with all aspects of the textile trade – raw materials, finished goods, printing, dyeing, wholesaling and retailing. It was the largest cotton market in the world. The focus of all this activity was the Exchange, its trading floor extended again and again to cope with an ever increasing volume of business. Close to the Exchange, and also to the hotels where the outside traders stayed, were the commercial warehouses, developed in Manchester as a unique building type. They were a combination of showroom, storehouse and shipping depot, with their own specialised machinery and their own architectural traditions. As trading took over, so the mills, which at first had dominated the Manchester skyline, moved ever further out from the centre into the surrounding countryside and to the towns of South Lancashire beyond.

By 1861 when the *Building News* ran an article on Manchester, the face of the city was transformed. "Manchester is a more interesting city to walk over than London," the magazine commented. "One can scarcely walk about Manchester without coming across frequent examples of the grand in architecture. There has been nothing to equal it since the building of Venice." Modern warehouses, banks, offices, theatres, clubs, shops and hotels lined the streets of the city centre, replacing the jumble of houses, workshops and mills of the modest Georgian town. The new industrial magnates were concerned to make a show and believed in spending money on architectural display. Their warehouses were modelled on Renaissance palazzi, dignified and solidly built. Their banks were ostentatious, with interiors lined in marble and bronze. But three great public buildings, each by local architects, sum up the High Victorian period. The Free Trade Hall of 1856 by Edward Walters was dedicated not to a saint like St George's Hall, Liverpool, or to royalty like the Albert Hall, but to an economic theory – Free Trade – and on its proud facade are sculpted ladies seated amidst cog-wheels, boilers, ships and cotton bales. The Albert Memorial, completed in 1867 by Thomas Worthington, pre-dated George Gilbert Scott's more famous London monument in its use of a Gothic shrine as a setting for a statue of the Prince Consort. But the greatest symbol of Manchester's economic power and success was the Town Hall by Alfred Waterhouse, a municipal palace in the style of a medieval Flemish cloth hall, with suites of specially designed furniture, lavish decorations and murals by Ford Madox Brown.

The spirit of liberal nonconformism, which was such a potent force in Victorian Manchester, is expressed most clearly in the buildings of Thomas Worthington. His interest in the problems of urban society and his pioneering work in the design of hospitals, workers' housing and public baths placed him at the forefront of progressive social practice. He captured the mood of the time too in the presidential address he gave to the Manchester Society of Architects in 1875: "Manchester is acquiring a reputation of a town of some architectural character; it is the inland metropolis of the North, the Florence, if I may so describe it, of the nineteenth century; it has developed a style of architecture which we may largely call our own, and in which we may take a not unnatural pride."

The merchant princes for whom this architecture was created moved their places of residence gradually further and further from the centre. In the 18th century Mosley Street was the most fashionable address but by 1839 it had become an area of commercial warehouses. The first migrants moved to large terraced houses at the Crescent in Salford and to Ardwick or Chorlton-on-Medlock. In 1835 Victoria Park was laid out in Rusholme with detached villas in spacious grounds, and later suburbs sprang up around the southern boundaries of the city, far enough from the smoke to enjoy the wholesome country air, but within easy drive of the banks and warehouses. With the development of the railways, commuting became easier and wealthy industrialists moved out to savour the country life in Cheshire. By the end of the century the city centre had been abandoned to commerce and the zone around it to densely packed streets of working class housing.

By the 1870s Manchester was facing increased competition from textile centres in Germany and America. Britain's balance of trade as a whole had declined, and the city's businessmen searched for new markets, installed improved technology and cut prices to stave off stagnation. The Ship Canal offered a daring opportunity for economic revival and captured the public imagination. Seventeen thousand men were engaged in its construction which took seven years, and the canal opened in 1894. It was not a financial success, but by providing a direct link with international markets, it made possible the expansion of new industries such as heavy engineering and chemicals. Although some of the most spectacular textile warehouses date from the Edwardian period and business on the Exchange continued to expand, the early 20th century saw the start of the inexorable decline in the city's dependence upon cotton.

The atmosphere of Manchester in its heyday is still to be found in the centre of the city, its streets enlivened with the picturesque and decorative detail of its Victorian buildings; even the names are redolent of those times – Orient House, Asia House, Bombay Street, Dantzic Street. In spite of the terrible destruction of war and of brutal 1960s redevelopment, the achievements of Victorian and Edwardian architects still give the city a distinct identity. In the areas around Princess Street and Whitworth Street can be seen block upon block of dignified warehouses, unified in scale, built of a common range of materials, and subtly detailed. Dominating the skyline of the now depressed industrial satellites stand churches of striking beauty. In the bustling streets of the commercial districts are banks and clubs, offices and shops, theatres and hotels reminding us that Manchester was a place not only of power and wealth, but a city with a clear vision of its cultural identity. This book is a celebration of "the most wonderful city of modern times."

Acknowledgements

This book is a portrait of Victorian buildings in Manchester and Salford as they now stand. Many individuals, companies and institutions have been generous in assisting this project, especially in permitting access for photographs and supplying information about buildings. In particular the following are thanked: Robin Bluhm, Ivan Biggs, Christopher Bourne, Lucia Crothall, Angela Darvill, Peter Helm, Dr M. A. Pegg, Ian Pringle, David Rhodes, William Shawcross, Neil Wilkie and the staff of the Viewpoint Photography Gallery, Salford; the Church of St Augustine, Pendlebury; Hyde's Anvil Brewery; the Lamb, Eccles; Manchester City Council; the Royal Exchange Theatre Company; Salford City Council; the Victoria Theatre, Salford; Whitbread and Company. Mike Williams of the Greater Manchester Archaeological Unit provided information on mills. Julian Treuherz read the draft text and made valuable suggestions. Ryburn Publishing Limited expresses gratitude to the John Rylands University Library of Manchester for permission to publish photographs of the library. Ian Beesley wishes to acknowledge the generous assistance of Ilford Ltd in supplying photographic materials. Finally we would like to express our thanks to Richard Clark of Ryburn Publishing for his unfailing commitment to this project.

Bibliography

In recent years much new information has been published on 19th century Manchester and Salford. In spite of this the best general book on the city's architecture remains 'The Stones of Manchester' by Cecil Stewart, 1956. Other valuable books on the subject include 'Guide Across Manchester' by Philip Atkins, revised edition 1987; 'Some Manchester Streets and Their Buildings' by C. H. Reilly, 1924; 'South Lancashire' (Buildings of England series) by Nikolaus Pevsner, 1969; 'Art and Architecture in Victorian Manchester' edited by John Archer, 1985; and 'Thomas Worthington' by Anthony J. Pass, 1988.

Note

Would readers please note that in this book the term Victorian has been used somewhat loosely to include the period up to 1914.

The introductory photographs include subjects outside this period.

An alphabetical index of the photographs appears at the end of the book. As far as possible, in the captions accompanying the photographs we have given each building the name most likely to help a visitor find it, the address, the architects and the year of opening.

1. Knolls House, Bury New Road, Salford *(moved from Market Street and re-erected for William Yates, 1822; demolished 1988)*

2. Manchester Carriage and Tramways Company Depot, Bury New Road, Salford *(about 1875; demolished 1988)*

3. Park Villa, Great Clowes Street, Salford *(about 1840)*

4. Church of St Mark, Cheetham Hill Road *(1794 and 1855)*

5. Victoria Bridge, Cateaton Street *(1839)*

6. Wharf at Victoria and Albert Warehouses *(about 1840)*

7. CWS Food Packing Factory, Pollard Street *(about 1910)*

8. Working Girls Home, Little Nelson Street *(1890s)*

9. River Irwell

10. Newton Silk Mill, Newton Heath *(1832)*

11. Redhill Street Mills, Ancoats *(1790 to 1912)*
In 1825 the great German neo-classical architect Karl Friedrich Schinkel visited Manchester and sketched McConnel and Kennedy's mill in Redhill Street. "The enormous factory buildings are seven to eight storeys high," he wrote. "One sees buildings where, three years ago, there were only meadows, but the buildings are so black that they look as if they have been used for one hundred years." Alexis de Tocqueville singled out the mill for concerned comment in 1835: "1,500 workers labouring 69 hours a week. Average of wages: 11 shillings a week.... Three quarters of the workers in Messrs Connel's factory are women or children." James McConnel and John Kennedy, two self-made Scotsmen, erected their spinning mill in 1818, alongside the earlier Murray's Mill which appears on the right in the photograph above. Eight storeys high, it was one of the tallest iron framed buildings in the world. The early years of Victoria's reign were lean times for the cotton industry but in 1851 the company acquired patent rights for Heilmann's new combing machine which enabled them to prosper even during the cotton famine of the American Civil War. In 1865 the mill was altered by Sir William Fairbairn to accommodate the larger self-acting spinning mules which he had invented. Already the biggest mill complex in Manchester, it continued to grow; an L-shaped wing was added at the rear in 1868 and two further buildings in 1912. Together these mills form a sheer cliff of plain brickwork. Though no longer humming with the activity of cotton production, on winter evenings they can still evoke the sight which so impressed Disraeli's Coningsby, of "illuminated factories with more windows than Italian palaces and smoking chimneys taller than Egyptian obelisks."

12. Victoria Mills, Varley Street, Miles Platting *(1867 and 1873)*
In the Victorian period Manchester was no longer a mill town but a city of warehousing. The Georgian mills with their smoking chimneys were swept away in the movement to build warehouses. But on the eastern edge of the city some new cotton spinning mills were constructed and one of the largest was the Victoria Mills at Miles Platting. This great six storey complex was erected for William Holland who had forsaken a site at the Adelphi in Salford because of flooding and chosen a prime position on the Rochdale Canal. The mill was built in two phases, in 1867 and 1873, and consists of two identical blocks joined by an engine house. The most striking feature is the tall chimney, a mighty shaft rising from an octagonal drum, its base pierced by arcading. The architect was possibly George Woodhouse of Bolton who designed similar structures in the Italianate style. The mill was worked until 1960 but now it is empty, a great hulk stranded in the wastelands of East Manchester.

13. Victoria and Albert Warehouses, Water Street *(about 1840)*
The River Irwell and the Mersey into which it flows were improved in the 1730s so that ships from Warrington and Liverpool could sail up to Manchester. The river remained in use long after the completion of the Bridgewater Canal in 1765. In the 1840s a number of warehouses were built on the river front, including the Victoria and Albert Warehouses which occupied the site of the open quay after which Quay Street was named. With their rows of small windows and limited headroom these buildings continue the form of the earlier Merchants' Warehouse and Middle Warehouse at the Castlefield Canal Basin. In 1839 the Irwell was connected to the Rochdale Canal by the construction of the Manchester and Salford Junction Canal, and the remains of the entrance lock are still visible close to the Victoria Warehouse. The canal ran under the present site of the Granada TV building through a tunnel 500 yards long. The Victoria and Albert Warehouses now form part of Granada's empire and are used for storage and filming but their interiors are largely unaltered.

14

15

16 *(see overleaf)*

14. The Packet House, Bridgewater Canal Basin, Worsley *(about 1850)*
The Bridgewater Canal was constructed in 1761 by James Brindley for Francis Egerton, 3rd Duke of Bridgewater. It carried coal to Manchester from the mines at Worsley and heralded the start of the canal age. At Worsley Delph, just past the Packet House, is the entrance to the mines: a network of underground canals stretching 46 miles was constructed on two levels connected by an inclined plane. In 1769 a passenger service to Manchester was introduced with a landing stage and ticket office at Castlefield. The landing steps remain at Worsley in front of the Packet House. The programme of development was continued by Francis Leveson-Gower, later 1st Earl of Ellesmere, who inherited the estate. He built the Court House in 1849 and added the picturesque timber-framed wing onto the 18th century Packet House, both very early examples of the black and white revival. In 1851 Queen Victoria and Prince Albert visited Worsley, travelling by canal from Patricroft on a specially built barge. The Queen was impressed, recording that "the boat glided along in a most noiseless and dreamlike manner amidst the cheers of the people," but the cheers frightened one of the horses towing the Royal Barge and caused it to fall into the canal. In the later 19th century, competition from the railways was too great and the transport of coal ceased in 1887. Today the canal basin has been restored, though minerals from the underground mines which feed it have tinted the water the colour of tomato soup.

15. Barton Bridge and Aqueduct, Manchester Ship Canal, Barton *(Sir William Leader, 1893)*
The Ship Canal was built between 1887 and 1894 and made Manchester into a major port by enabling steamships to by-pass Liverpool and sail direct to the new docks at Salford. In addition to forming cuttings and locks, the operation involved constructing new railway and swing road bridges and, in the case of the Bridgewater Canal, the famous swing aqueduct. The canal formerly crossed the River Irwell at Barton by James Brindley's equally notable 600 foot stone aqueduct, the abutments of which remain on the northern bank. The present aqueduct which replaced it in 1893 was designed by Sir Leader Williams and consists of a 235 feet long iron trough with gates to retain the water. Like the wrought iron road bridge, it swings on a central axis to allow the passage of ships, driven on roller bearings by hydraulic engines. On an island between the two structures is the central control tower which contains the operating machinery, engines and pumps, much of it dating from the opening of the canal.

16 and 17. Castlefield Railway Viaduct *(Sacré, Johnson and A. Johnstone, 1877)*

The Castlefield area is sliced up by successive transport networks. First came the canals: both the Bridgewater and the Rochdale Canals terminate at the Castlefield Basin. The world's first passenger railway station opened in 1830 at Liverpool Road; its hinterland developed thereafter for goods warehousing. In 1849 a great brick viaduct leading to Oxford Road Station was built alongside the Rochdale Canal for the Manchester, South Junction and Altrincham Railway.

But the most dramatic and also most devastating construction was the approach to Central Station. 1,200 people lost their homes for the building of the station and its tracks, the giant legs of the iron viaduct striding through the densely populated area on its relentless path towards the city centre. Remains of the Roman Fort were smashed in the process, though in deference to the shattered fragment, the viaduct was dressed up with towers and crenellations. Where it crossed the Bridgewater Canal an immense bridge of lattice girders was constructed with twin spans of 145 and 203 feet. When the Great Northern Railway Goods Warehouse was erected in 1898, the viaduct was widened on the north side to take four tracks, and a new spur built across Deansgate. Since the closure of Central Station in 1969 no trains have run along the viaduct but under plans for the city's new Light Rapid Transit system it may be re-opened to take trams into G-Mex from the Altrincham line.

18. G-Mex Centre, Windmill Street *(Sir John Fowler with Sacré, Johnson and A. Johnstone, 1880)*
Central Station, Manchester's fourth and last railway terminus, was built for three companies – the
Midland, the Great Northern, and the Manchester, Sheffield and Lincolnshire Railways – which
together formed the Cheshire Lines Committee. It came closest to the city centre and resulted in the
construction of an arched train shed exceeded in span only by that of St Pancras, the Midland's London
terminus. The massive iron and glass structure sits on a vaulted brick undercroft, a continuation of the
viaduct which brought the trains in at high level through Castlefield. The great scale of the arched roof
has always been a dominant feature of the city as the hotel projected to stand in front of the train shed was
never built. In 1969, as a result of the Beeching axe, the station closed and for many years the train shed
deteriorated, its platforms used for car parking. There were many changes of ownership before
eventually it was acquired by Greater Manchester County Council. Its conversion to an exhibition centre
was one of the greatest achievements of that short-lived local authority.

19. Midland Hotel, St Peter's Square *(Charles Trubshaw, 1903)*
When Central Station was opened in 1880 the Midland Railway Company intended to screen the end of the great train shed with a new hotel as at St Pancras, the other terminus on their London to Manchester line. Due to shortage of funds the project faltered and it was not until 1898 that they began construction on an adjacent site. Once started there was no skimping: the hotel had a palm court, a concert hall, winter gardens, Russian and Turkish baths, Parisian milliners, a roof garden, 23 lifts, three and a half miles of corridors and 400 bedrooms. Occupying two acres and rising to 10 storeys, it is an extravaganza in shiny glazed brick, terracotta and polished granite which glistens in the late afternoon light. But it was also technologically advanced, one of the first steel-framed buildings in Britain, with an air filtration system to protect its guests against the smoky Manchester atmosphere. On opening, the building was described as "colossal in size, striking in magnificence...probably the most beautiful building in the whole city." If beauty equals quantity of ornamentation, then this is possibly so, but its eclectic mixture of Renaissance motifs is the kind of Victorian architecture which fell deeply into disfavour in the post war period and internally it suffered from crude and insensitive alterations. Now, after a fashion, it has been restored, and if one looks inside there are original features: marble corridors, shiny walnut panelling, decorative plaster ceilings, and the splendid French restaurant.

20 and 21. Victoria Station, Victoria Station Approach *(William Dawes, 1904)*
Victoria Station opened in 1844 as the terminus for the Manchester and Leeds Railway; the first buildings were by George Stephenson and they partly survive on Hunts Bank. Forty years later Exchange Station was built alongside by the London and North Western Railway, so producing the famous combined platform 2,194 feet long and allowing trains to pass through Manchester from Liverpool to Leeds. A series of extensions was built at Victoria so that by the turn of the century the station was dealing with 700 trains and 40,000 passengers a day. In 1903 work started on the present station buildings which were designed by William Dawes. Eventually 17 platforms were built, taking passengers bound for Yorkshire, Scotland and Blackpool, as well as to the cotton towns on the northern and eastern fringes of the city. The delicate glass and iron canopy sheltering the pavement outside tempts the traveller with the names of one-time destinations from Bolton to Belgium. There are good interiors too: the restaurant with coloured glass and a dome bulging with fruits, the panelled booking hall, and a map of the Lancashire and Yorkshire Railway system in white tiles. One feature that has disappeared is the overhead baggage railway. This ran at roof level and transported an electric trolley carrying a huge basket which could be lowered onto each platform. Opposite the station building until 1978 was the impressive stone frontage of the L & Y's parcels office which was shamefully demolished to provide an unflattering back view of Chetham's School.

20

22. London Warehouse, Ducie Street *(1867)*

Piccadilly Station, originally called London Road, was opened by the Manchester and Birmingham Railway Company in 1842. Shortly afterwards it was also used by the Manchester, Sheffield and Lincolnshire Railway, and in 1865-66 a new joint station was developed, with each company having separate platforms and passenger facilities. In 1867 the MS & LR put up the monumental London Warehouse, the only survivor of four large warehouses built close to the station. It is seven storeys high, its scale emphasized by vertical brick panels punched out with arched windows and huge stone quoins rising up at each corner. Its structure followed the latest theories on fireproof construction: massive cast iron columns supporting wrought box girders and brick arched floors. The wrought iron girders had greater tensile strength than cast iron and allowed wider spacing of columns to permit easier movement of cloth bales. The warehouse was reached by a branch track which ran alongside the station and over Store Street. In constructing this, part of the Ashton Canal Basin was filled in, expressing the supremacy of rail over water for transport of goods. But today the tracks have gone and the railway has been converted into a car park, whilst the canal, though not navigable, still survives.

23. Great Northern Railway Company Goods Warehouse, Watson Street *(1898)*

The GNR Goods Warehouse rises high above the surrounding streets and proclaims its company name in large letters of white brick below the cornice line. It was built late in the history of Manchester's railway developments, but brought new technical sophistication to the storage and handling of goods. The warehouse provided an interchange between rail, canal and road. In a tunnel underneath the building ran the Manchester and Salford Junction Canal. Hoists connected this to the goods station at two levels inside the building. The railway came in on a viaduct from the tracks leading into Central Station, and opened out into an immense area of marshalling yards raised up on a platform in front of the warehouse. Access up from street level was by ramps with hydraulic haulage. Square steel columns support rivetted steel beams and brick arches, allowing much greater spans and fewer columns than an iron structure. Along the Deansgate frontage is a long narrow range of shops and offices screening the marshalling yards and recording the names of places served by the company. The warehouse is now used as a car park but there are plans to reuse it in connection with the neighbouring G-Mex Centre.

25. Princess Street Warehouses *(photograph overleaf)*

The commercial warehouse was Victorian Manchester's speciality. As the *Manchester Critic* wrote in 1871, "The architectural quality of the town is mainly derived from these buildings." The finest spectacle was Portland Street, where block after block of impressive warehouses of regular height and proportion stretched into the far distance. Portland Street has suffered war damage and redevelopment, but an idea of the grand effect which so impressed 19th century visitors can be gained by looking along Princess Street. Like the great palazzi flanking the Via del Corso in Rome, each warehouse has rows of regular windows, a central doorway, and at the top an emphatic cornice. The principal floor is always raised above street level, reached by a set of steps. The lower basement generally contained the machinery — steam engines and boilers which powered the hoists and the packing presses above. These compressed the bales of cloth before they were bound and dispatched. The main counting house and offices were on the ground floor. A central staircase would then lead to the upper floors where each department had its sample rooms with storage to the rear. Although buying was done at the Exchange, visitors were invited to inspect goods in the warehouses and the cloth was arranged on mahogany counters below the windows of the upper floors. As loading was not permitted from the street, each warehouse had its hovel or gated cartway and loading area. Such functional requirements produced a specialised building type but the need to impress buyers encouraged architectural display and the result was very different from the utilitarian mills where the cloth was produced.

24. Britannia Hotel, Portland Street *(Travis and Mangnall, 1858)*
This spectacular building was erected for S. & J. Watts, the largest wholesale drapery business in Manchester. It is the most ambitious and showy of all the city's Victorian warehouses. James Watts, the chief proprietor, was the classic type of Manchester entrepreneur; son of a self-made man, a free-trader and a dissenter. He was concerned not only with business success but also to make a social mark, and at his country house, Abney Hall, Cheadle, he welcomed leading politicians, bishops and aristocrats. Even Prince Albert stayed with him whilst visiting Manchester to open the 1857 Art Treasures Exhibition. His immense warehouse exemplifies this self-confident spirit with its cavalier mixture of styles and details. Whilst the overall framework is Italianate, the windows of each storey are given a different treatment: Italian Renaissance, Elizabethan, French Renaissance, Flemish, and then at the top, instead of a projecting cornice, four towers rise forth lit by great Gothic rose windows. Along the parapet and on the tops of the towers was formerly a cresting of curved gables enriched with urns, presenting a skyline like a gigantic jewelled crown. The warehouse was built to impress buyers from all over the world, and, once inside, the visitor was led by a splendid iron staircase to floors filled with fabrics, furnishings, clothing and all manner of drapery. The building closed in 1972 and narrowly avoided demolition. As the Britannia Hotel it enjoys a brashness and glitter well suited to its reputation as the queen of Manchester warehouses.

26. The Textile Institute, Blackfriars Street, Salford *(F. H. Oldham, 1884)*
One of the most individual of warehouse buildings is just on the Salford side of the River Irwell. It was built for Baerlein and Company by the Manchester architect F. H. Oldham. The stone facade, recently cleaned, is a curious mixture of High Victorian Gothic and Queen Anne. Pointed arched windows sit within Norman Shaw type oriels, and Gothic shafts rise up into Flemish gables. But it is all done with verve and shows the degree of eclectic brainstorming to which Victorian architects went to achieve originality. It makes a striking contrast with the neighbouring Venetian Gothic facade of No 16, erected in 1866 for de Jersey and Company.

25

26

27. Fraser House, Charlotte Street *(Edward Walters, 1855)*
One of the best concentrations of palazzo style warehouses is in Charlotte Street, just off Portland Street. Charlotte House, Austin House, 34 Charlotte Street and Fraser House were all designed by Edward Walters and erected between 1855 and 1860. The application of the palazzo style to Manchester's warehouses was initiated by Walters and this group shows the variations which were possible within the Italianate theme. No 34 is the simplest, its plain rows of windows closely spaced to admit maximum light for viewing the textiles. In contrast, Austin House and Charlotte House are richly decorated with a strong cornice, carved doorcase and stone base. Fraser House has a powerful rhythm of round arches, subtly different on each floor. The amount of ornamentation depended upon the budget, but as long as the proportions and details were correctly Italianate, a dignified effect was achieved. In Reyner Street at the side of Fraser House, and in Back George Street, where the facades are strictly utilitarian, can still be seen the hovels or off-street loading bays into which a horse and cart could be backed. In these narrow streets it is easy to imagine the clatter of iron wheels on stone setts and the cries of the warehousemen loading the carts high with bales of cloth.

28. 41-43 Faulkner Street *(Thomas F. Taylor, 1846)*
A warehouse which predates the Charlotte Street group is just round the corner at 41-43 Faulkner Street. Its architect, Thomas Taylor, shunned the palazzo style, first introduced by Walters in 1839, and chose to express the narrow frontage of his building in the full dress style of the Greek Revival. On a tall base of rock-faced stone stands a giant order of Doric columns supporting a pediment with the windows fitted between. The architectural result is not altogether a success, for the multi-storey warehouse is very different in form to a Greek temple. But it is a robust and engaging design, which clamours for attention amongst the bustle of Chinatown.

29. Tootal, Broadhurst and Lee Building, Oxford Street *(J. Gibbon Sankey, 1898)*
The headquarters of two of the country's largest textile companies used to face one another across
Oxford Street. Tootal's warehouse of 1898 was the earlier; the other, reflected in this photograph, was St
James's House by Clegg, Fryer and Penman built in 1912 for the Calico Printers Association. Now both
are part of the Courtauld Group and the two buildings are leased as offices. St James's House is a great
cliff of Portland stone, aggrandised with Baroque keystones and curved pediments. It contains over 1000
rooms. Tootals is more individual in pink brick and stripey terracotta. On the corner of Great
Bridgewater Street two beefy men crouch over a window straining to support the upper floors. Further
down Great Bridgewater Street is Lee House, built as an extension in 1931 by Harry S. Fairhurst and
Son. Its stylish modernistic design in steel and glass was worked up from a drawing by the progressive
Manchester architect James Henry Sellers for a seventeen storey skyscraper, but only the first eight floors
were built. It was one of the last textile warehouses to be erected in Manchester.

30, 33 and 34. Refuge Assurance Building, Oxford Street *(Alfred Waterhouse, 1891)*
Just short of its centenary, the Refuge Assurance Company has forsaken its great flagship for new premises in suburban Wilmslow. The Refuge Building is now empty. It is a huge pile of hot red terracotta and pressed brick, erected in three stages. The original block of 1891 designed by Alfred Waterhouse is on the corner of Whitworth Street and Oxford Street (34, overleaf); the tower and extension along Oxford Street date from 1910 by his son Paul; and the Whitworth Street extension by Stanley Birkett was added as recently as the 1930s (33, overleaf). The tower is a great landmark, visible from afar. Its strong modelling and flat surfaces contrast with the two blocks it seeks to unite, prompting the architect Professor C. H. Reilly to describe it as "like a tall young man in flannel trousers escorting two charming, but somewhat delicate old ladies dressed in lace." The blocks are ornamented with a profusion of intricate detail, not showy but well mannered and discreet. Inside are lofty spaces lined in white and yellow tiles and divided by polished mahogany screens. The 1930s extension, whilst all red terracotta on the outside, is built of reinforced concrete and houses a large hall with a sprung floor, fully equipped as a theatre for company entertainments.

31 and 32. Lancaster House and India House, Whitworth Street *(Harry S. Fairhurst, 1906)*
The completion of the Ship Canal in 1894 made Manchester a great export centre and revived, briefly, the construction of warehouses. Whereas in the past textile merchants each had their own warehouse, it had become more convenient for several export companies to share packing facilities and equipment in one single building. New materials and technology permitted taller buildings and a concentration of these giants gives Whitworth Street its exhilarating character.

Whitworth Street was formed in 1899 as part of a proposed ring road following the line of the elevated Manchester, South Junction and Altrincham Railway which connects Oxford Road and Piccadilly Stations. Viewed from the street, these huge buildings of granite, brick and decorative orange terracotta rear up to exclude the sky, but seen from the railway viaduct at the back, they present great walls of steel and glass, modern and functional-looking in their lack of any historical dress. It was their efficiency which impressed contemporary critics, and with India House and Lancaster House Harry Fairhurst made his reputation as the leading designer of modern warehouses. Though long empty and neglected, both buildings are now being converted to flats as part of an ambitious scheme to revitalise the Whitworth Street area.

33

34

35. Royal Bank of Scotland, St Ann Street (*J. E. Gregan, 1849*)

St Ann's Square was still partly residential when Benjamin Heywood built this bank. His father and uncle had bought a house occupying the site in 1796 and used it as both home and bank. The bank was successful and Heywood was able to enjoy a different style of life. He moved out to a large villa on the Eccles Old Road, became an M.P. in 1831, and was made a baronet in 1837. He was a philanthropist and a founder member of the Royal Manchester Institution. His new bank, designed by the talented young architect John Edgar Gregan, was a most discerning commission. The building is divided into two elements linked by an arched entrance: a tall stone block and a smaller brick part. In the latter were domestic offices and in the former was the banking hall with the safes below and the principal rooms of the manager's residence above. It is the skilful way in which these two blocks of differing heights are united that is so satisfying and such a lesson in good street architecture. The bank is in the palazzo style and the brick block is very much in the manner of Barry's Travellers' Club, London. But the taller block is most individual with great rusticated Venetian windows, a chamfered corner and deliberate contrasts of scale and texture. Gregan took great trouble with the quarrying and laying of the stonework so that it would not suffer from premature erosion, and indeed it still retains its razor sharp crispness which accentuates the complex patterns of tooling and rustication. With the Free Trade Hall and the Mosley Street branch of the Royal Bank of Scotland, it is one of the three great buildings of the Renaissance style in Manchester.

36. Royal Bank of Scotland, Mosley Street *(Edward Walters, 1860)*

In the late 18th century Mosley Street was the most fashionable residential address in Manchester. The street was lined with handsome Georgian houses and the building of the Portico Library and the Royal Manchester Institution in the early years of the 19th century only increased its attraction. But then around 1835 commerce arrived and the houses were gradually demolished. One of the first commercial buildings was erected for the Manchester and Salford Bank and has a handsome facade with a giant order. Standing next to Lewis's it is now used by the Bradford and Bingley Building Society. In 1862 the Manchester and Salford moved down the street to larger premises, in the grandest of all High Victorian bank buildings. It is the last great work of Edward Walters and confirms his superb mastery of the palazzo style. All surfaces are richly modelled: rusticated ground floor, a piano nobile with pedimented windows and an elaborate cornice and balustrade surmounted by urns. The huge portal on Mosley Street is part of the original design, but the smaller block beyond is an extension of the 1880s by Barker and Ellis who had continued Walters' practice. The Manchester and Salford became Williams Deacon's and is now the Royal Bank of Scotland.

37. 1-3 York Street *(Charles Heathcote, 1902)*
One of the most prolific of Manchester architects, and also amongst the most talented, was Charles Henry Heathcote. He commenced practice in Manchester in 1872 and established a solid reputation as a designer of banks and office blocks. This is his best building, erected for Parr's Bank on the corner of York Street and Spring Gardens. It exploits the site to advantage, thrusting out at the corner with angle turrets and a large dome. In contrast to the surrounding buildings, it is faced in dark red sandstone, a material well suited to its enjoyable display of pomp and grandeur. All sorts of Baroque tricks are brought out: exaggerated keystones, block rustication, obelisks, pedimented dormers, and, most wilful of all, rows of paired columns like fat legs, supporting nothing more than giant scrolls. Inside is a splendid banking hall lined in coloured marbles. In 1972 the City Council gave consent for demolition of the building, but after a lengthy campaign by the Victorian Society in which over 11,000 signatures were collected urging that it be saved, the owners were persuaded to change their plans. Now it is being converted into a club.

38. 46-48 Brown Street *(George Truefitt, 1868)*

One of the wealthiest of Manchester's Victorian entrepreneurs was Sir William Cunliffe Brooks. His grandfather William had established a bank in Blackburn, and under the next two generations the family business boomed. Sir William, born in 1819, had houses in London, the Highlands of Scotland and the Mediterannean, as well as Barlow Hall in Chorlton-cum-Hardy, Manchester. 46-48 Brown Street is what remains of his opulent Manchester bank. Brooks Bank originally stretched through from Chancery Lane to King Street where Ship Canal House now stands. Outside the Chancery Lane entrance was a massive porte-cochère and a forecourt enclosed by high iron railings. The splendid top-lit banking hall was lined in Siena marble and divided by gilt columns and brass screens. When built in 1868 the bank was admired: "The style is really original," wrote *The Builder,* "showing in a successful combination some of the best characteristics both of Gothic and Italian design." The surviving part, formerly called Lombard Chambers, was built as the bank offices, with boldly textured stone walls overlayed by a mass of Gothic ornamentation. There are intricate flowers and rosettes carved by Williams and Mooney and prickly ironwork by Bellhouse of Manchester. Brooks, who became M.P. for East Cheshire in 1869, was one of the new breed of merchant princes who modelled their lives on the illustrious bankers of medieval and Renaissance Italy. His bank building was intended to evoke that tradition.

39. Trustee Savings Bank, King Street *(C. R. Cockerell, 1846)*

This was the first of three major provincial branches of the Bank of England erected in the 1840s by C. R. Cockerell. All were executed in a highly personal classical style. The facade to King Street is in the form of a Greek Doric temple front, but the temple is freely adapted to suit the needs of a commercial building without loss of architectural unity. Thus gravity is achieved through the use of a powerful order of unfluted columns, applied without structural purpose, whilst the pediment is lifted free of the entablature to allow the insertion of an upper storey. The three massive arched openings express the banking hall behind, the central one defining a tunnel vault which leads through to a saucer dome supported on cast iron columns. Entry was from the side street originally; the front entrance cut through the plinth is a later Victorian alteration. With this building, Cockerell went far beyond the conventional purity of the Greek Revival, imbuing the style with a vitality and stength absent in the work of earlier classical architects working in Manchester such as Richard Lane. But by the 1840s the Renaissance palazzo without an order had become the fashionable model in the city and Cockerell inspired no followers.

40. Theatre Royal, Peter Street *(Irwin and Chester, 1845)*
Peter Street, together with Oxford Street, was once Manchester's theatre district, home of the Gaiety, the Tivoli, the Grand and the Theatre Royal. Only the last of these remains, and it is the city's oldest surviving theatre. It was erected after the destruction by fire in 1844 of Manchester's second Theatre Royal in Fountain Street. Its manager John Knowles bought the rights and decided to rebuild on the new site in Peter Street. The building has a splendid monumental facade of painted stone with giant fluted Corinthian columns supporting a great entablature and pediment. Sheltering under the portico is a marble statue of Shakespeare propping himself up on one elbow. The theatre cost £23,000 to build and included the precautionary device of a 20,000 gallon water tank placed on the roof and connected by pipes to the stage and green room in case of fire. In its heyday there appeared on the stage the likes of William Macready, Henry Irving, Edmund Keen, Helen Faucit and Jenny Lind. The interior was altered in 1875 by Edward Salomons who improved the seating, refreshment rooms and stage facilities. In 1923 it became a cinema and then in 1972 a Bingo Hall. Now it is empty, and current plans for conversion to a night club will complete the fall from grace.

41. Royal Exchange, St Ann's Square *(Mills and Murgatroyd, 1874)*
Until the 1930s the focus of Manchester's commercial life was the Exchange and Manchester itself was at the centre of the most important cotton industry in the world. At its peak the Exchange had a membership of 11,000 and twice weekly the Great Hall was filled with a throng of traders buying and selling cotton and everything associated with its production. The first Exchange of 1729 was a room over the market hall but this was replaced in 1809 with a new building by Thomas Harrison of Chester in the Grecian style at its most severe. During the 19th century the trading floor was repeatedly enlarged to meet the demands of business. In 1836 and 1845 large extensions were built and then in the 1870s a new building, two and a half times the size, was erected by Mills and Murgatroyd in an overblown classical style. Even this proved insufficient and the Exchange was again enlarged during the years of the First World War by the Bolton firm of Bradshaw, Gass and Hope. The heyday was shortlived: between the wars the industry declined and when the building was damaged in the blitz, half the trading floor was closed down and converted into offices. But what remains is still a gargantuan marble hall, a monument to the age of cotton. Following the closure of the Exchange in 1968, the Great Hall has found a new purpose. With the brilliant installation of an angular steel and glass auditorium for the Royal Exchange Theatre Company, the former trading floor has become a focus of Manchester's cultural life.

42. Free Trade Hall, Peter Street *(Edward Walters, 1856)*

The Free Trade Hall commemorates the part played by Manchester in the struggle for the abolition of trade tariffs. From 1838 until the repeal of the Corn Laws in 1846, Manchester was the headquarters of the free trade movement. Land for a meeting hall was given by one of its leaders, Richard Cobden, at St Peter's Fields, site of the 'Peterloo massacre' of 1819. A timber pavilion was constructed in 1840, replaced three years later by a plain brick building. Then in 1853 Edward Walters was selected to design a permanent hall. It is his greatest work and marks the supreme achievement of the Manchester palazzo style. In contrast with the multi-storey warehouses which formed his main output, Walters' design for the Free Trade Hall is a monumental composition with true Renaissance weight and gravity.

Integral to the rich modelling of the facade is decorative carving and a series of bold sculptures. In the spandrels of the ground floor arcade are shields of the Lancashire towns which took part in the Anti-Corn Law movement, and above the windows of the piano nobile are carved figures by John Thomas of London representing the Arts, Commerce, Manufacture, Agriculture, the Continents and, in the centre, Free Trade. The building suffered serious war damage and was reconstructed in 1950-51; of the original interior nothing remains. Amongst the users of the building, most famous is the Hallé orchestra which first performed in the hall in 1858, two years after the opening.

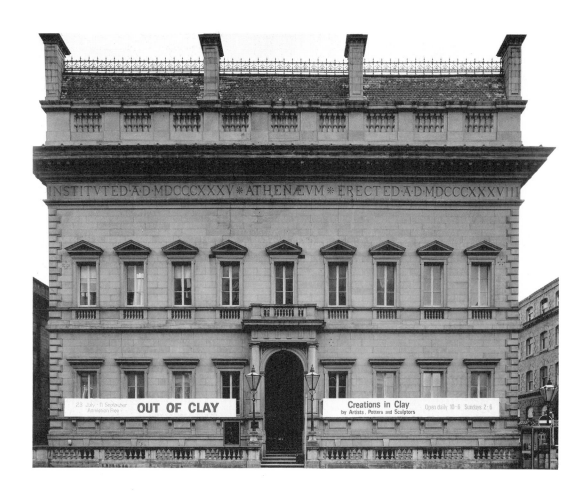

43. The Athenaeum Gallery, Princess Street *(Sir Charles Barry, 1839)*

The Manchester Athenaeum was founded in 1835 as a society devoted to the arts and learning. At first the members met in the premises of the Royal Manchester Institution but by the following year they had raised £10,000 by voluntary subscription and Charles Barry was commissioned to design a new building. Barry had designed the R.M.I. (now the City Art Gallery) in the Grecian style but for the Athenaeum he turned to the architecture of the Italian Renaissance. He had pioneered this style with the Travellers' Club in London, but its introduction to Manchester had far-reaching consequences for the architecture of the city. Urbane and sophisticated, this building dispensed with the classical orders and presented a two storey facade with large areas of flat stonework punctuated by regularly spaced windows, topped off by a projecting cornice. At the centre is an imposing doorcase reached by a tall flight of steps. Originally the building contained a library, newsroom, lecture hall and coffee room, and later a billiard room and gymnasium were created. Though at first there were financial problems, the Athenaeum soon became a centre for Manchester's literary life. In 1874 a fire destroyed the interior and, instead of rebuilding to the original roofline, a new lecture hall was provided by adding an extra storey. This accounts for the clumsy mansard roof which spoils the elegant proportions of the facade. The society survived until 1938 whereupon the building was taken over for government offices. It is now used for temporary exhibitions by the City Art Gallery next door.

44. Mechanics' Institute, Princess Street *(J. E. Gregan, 1856)*

The Manchester Mechanics' Institute was founded in 1824 and its first president was the banker and philanthropist Benjamin Heywood. By the 1850s the Institute had outgrown its premises in Cooper Street and funds were raised by public subscription for a new building in Princess Street (or David Street as it was then known). J. E. Gregan, who had already designed Heywood's Bank (now the Royal Bank of Scotland) in St Ann Street, was selected as architect. His design was for a three storey building in the palazzo style as with the bank, but without the refinement and surface detail. It is built of brick with stone dressings and has the regular, close spacing of windows seen in the surrounding warehouses; but examined more carefully it is clear that this is a most accomplished design, strong, handsome and well proportioned. Inside were provided a newsroom and reading room, with classrooms above and below. On the first floor was a great hall stretching the full width of the site and lit by huge triple arched windows. The tall parapet conceals an extra storey of classrooms added later. It was the last building to be designed by Gregan before he died in 1855 aged 42; indeed contemporary opinion held that misunderstandings over professional fees for the job hastened his death. In 1868 the first meeting of the Trades Union Congress was held in the building and this event has been its salvation. For years threatened with demolition, it is now owned by the City Council and is at last being restored as a museum of Labour History.

45. The Manchester Club (formerly Reform Club), King Street
(Edward Salomons and J. P. Jones, 1871)

In the 19th century Manchester was a centre of radical politics and progressive ideas. The Reform Club, founded in 1867, attracted many leading businessmen who established it as a rallying point for the Liberal Party. At first meetings were held in rented rooms above John Bright's warehouse in Spring Gardens but in 1871 a new building was erected round the corner in King Street. The club, seen on the left of the photograph, has a princely and exotic character. Its architect Edward Salomons was a versatile designer and here he chose to use the Venetian Gothic style. But it is an eclectic interpretation, mixing Venetian sources with steeply pitched Flemish roofs and strange angle turrets. Carved stonework writhes over the wall surfaces, jutting out into gargoyles and foliated capitals. The grand entrance is formed beneath a balcony used for speeches at election time. This originally led to a panelled staircase running up the full height of the building, for the ground floor was at first used as offices. Behind the tall arched windows on the first floor is a magnificent dining room, and above it is a billiard room large enough for four tables. Interior alterations in the mid 1890s included the creation of the splendid gentlemen's lavatories, all dark polished mahogany and green marble. In recent times the Reform Club was amalgamated and became the Manchester Club, but now it has been dissolved and the premises are empty. The other buildings in the photograph are Barclays Bank, built in 1890 by Heathcote and Rawle for the Lancashire and Yorkshire Bank, and 41 Spring Gardens, originally the National Provincial Bank, erected in the same year by Waterhouse. Their towers and gables form a romantic skyline at the top of King Street.

46. Albert Memorial, Albert Square *(Thomas Worthington, 1867)*
On the death of the Prince Consort in 1861, a memorial fund was launched in Manchester and suggestions invited for a suitable type of memorial. Ideas included public baths, botanical gardens and a school of science, but as the Mayor had already commissioned a statue of the Prince from Matthew Noble, it was decided that the funds should be used to provide a suitable setting for the sculpture. A design by Thomas Worthington was selected in which the statue was sheltered under a tall Gothic canopy as if in a shrine. It was a novel idea which Worthington had developed from a sketch he had made in 1848 of the Chapel of Santa Maria della Spina at Pisa and it predated Gilbert Scott's design for the more famous Albert Memorial in London. Worthington used the architectural setting for an elaborate display of sculpture and heraldry. At the base are the royal arms and crests of England and Saxony. In the niches of the four corner pinnacles are figures representing the interests of the Prince: Art holding a scroll and a pen, Commerce resting upon a ship's prow, Science and Agriculture. Within the spandrels of the tall gables are the heads of great artists and composers and on the pinnacles above are angels blowing trumpets. The Queen expressed approval of the design and on the presentation of the completed structure to the City of Manchester in 1867 the Mayor affirmed, "We accept it as a sacred charge and will preserve it with becoming care." This was not to be. By the 1970s it was in such poor condition that the City Council resolved to dismantle and sell it. Finally a Trust was established to raise funds to save the memorial and in 1978 Albert was restored.

47. Memorial Hall, Albert Square *(Thomas Worthington, 1866)*

Albert Square was created from 1864 as a setting for the Albert Memorial. One of the first buildings to front the new square was the Memorial Hall. The event it commemorates is the Act of Uniformity of 1662 which led to the ejection of 2,000 dissenting ministers from the Church of England and the beginning of nonconformity. The building provided a large public hall for educational activities as well as accommodation for social and philanthropic work. To produce an income, the lower floors were leased for warehousing. The architect Thomas Worthington fitted these functions into an awkward wedge-shaped site, placing the public hall on the top floor. For the exterior, Worthington chose the Venetian Gothic style which he had studied on a visit to Venice in 1858. Ruskin had praised the colour contrasts achieved by the use of natural materials in Venetian Gothic palazzi, and under his influence Worthington created a Manchester variation with vibrant banding in red, orange and black brickwork and buff stone. For the top floor he adopted the graceful window tracery of the Ca' d'Oro on the Grand Canal. The remainder of the south side of the square was constructed after the building of the Town Hall and, in deference to it, is in the Gothic style. Albert Chambers, next to the Memorial Hall, and the adjacent Carlton House are by Clegg and Knowles, and St Andrew's Chambers which turns the corner into Mount Street is by Waterhouse's pupil and son-in-law, George Redmayne. In the centre of the square, apart from the Albert Memorial, are four statues: John Bright, W. E. Gladstone, Oliver Heywood and Bishop Fraser. Radical politicians and enlightened benefactors of the Victorian age, they recall the heyday of Manchester liberalism and reform.

48-52. Town Hall, Albert Square *(Alfred Waterhouse, 1877)*

Manchester's first Town Hall in King Street lasted only 50 years. The rapid expansion of the city and the ambitions of its civic leaders led to the creation of a new municipal palace of unrivalled splendour. The architect Alfred Waterhouse was selected by competition in 1868. It was not a straightforward result; Waterhouse was placed first for his plan rather than for his external elevations, the submissions by Worthington and other finalists being considered more striking. But the efficiency, logic and simplicity of Waterhouse's scheme won the day and its inherent architectural qualities more than justified the decision. Waterhouse was a master of the Gothic style, having proved himself with the success of the Assize Courts at Strangeways built in 1864. The Town Hall is in the 13th century Gothic style, reminiscent of Flemish cloth halls, though the architect himself regarded it as "essentially 19th century...fitted to the wants of the present day." Placed on a triangular site, each elevation has a central feature, providing a loose symmetry to the overall design. But apart from the Albert Square frontage this is not readily apparent; from the side streets, only oblique views are possible where the projection and recession of the facades gives them a dynamic complexity. Dominating Albert Square is the majestic

48

clock tower, raised by 16 feet in the course of construction to perfect its proportions. In the manner of medieval buildings, the decoration inside and out incorporates reminders of the city's history. Around the exterior is a sequence of statues of Manchester worthies from Agricola, the Roman general in A.D. 59, to Thomas Potter, the first mayor in 1838.

Waterhouse exploited the triangular site to advantage by placing the Great Hall at the centre, separated from the perimeter offices by open courtyards. The state rooms are set out overlooking Albert Square. From the main entrance the visitor passes through a low vestibule flanked by sculptures of the Manchester scientists Dalton and Joule. This leads to twin ceremonial staircases which rise dramatically to the lobby of the Great Hall. Lobbies and corridors are faced in the hard, practical materials favoured by Waterhouse – mosaic floors, tiled walls and vivid polychrome stencilled ceilings. Incorporated in the design of these surfaces are bees and cotton strands, emblems of the city's industry. Waterhouse designed the decorations and furniture for the state rooms, frequently using stylised flower motifs in the manner of the Aesthetic Movement. A set of original curtains embroidered with sunflowers survives in the banqueting hall. In each room the wall is divided into oak panelled dado, wall panel and frieze. The wall panels were intended for mural paintings but these were never carried out. Only in the Great Hall was Waterhouse's idea of collaboration between architect and fine artist realised, in the exuberant series of mural paintings by Ford Madox Brown recording events in the history of Manchester. The huge wagon roof above glows richly with the gilded coats of arms of Manchester and its worldwide trading partners. In this hall, lit by the sparkling light of Gothic chandeliers, are embodied the ideals of the Victorian city – liberality, generosity, civic pride and municipal independence. Manchester's continuing spirit of radicalism is today symbolised by the act of covering the ceiling panel showing the arms of South Africa with the flag of the African National Congress.

49

51

53. Strangeways Prison, Southall Street *(Alfred Waterhouse, 1868)*
In 1859 an architectural competition for the design of new Manchester Assize Courts was won by the young Alfred Waterhouse. It established his reputation, bringing him renown and praise, and it also advanced the cause of those who favoured the Gothic style for public buildings. Before the courts were completed, Waterhouse was asked to design Strangeways Gaol on land immediately to the north east. The building was planned with separate men's and women's quarters, the men's having six wings radiating from a central hall and providing 912 cells, and the women's four wings with 380 cells. At the centre is a tall tower in the form of a minaret, visible from a wide surrounding area. This originally housed the water tanks, but was also used for ventilation and for observing the compound. The style of the buildings is Romanesque, heavy and intimidating, with high walls banded in brick and stone. The gatehouse in Southall Street provides the only entrance, its doorway surmounted by the Royal Arms and flanked by octagonal towers. The Assize Courts were demolished after war damage; the site is now a wasteland. But the prison is still in use, a grim reminder of Victorian penal conditions.

54 and 55. City Police Courts, Minshull Street *(Thomas Worthington, 1873)*
The competition for the design of new Manchester Police and Sessions Courts coincided with the great Town Hall competition, and Thomas Worthington and Alfred Waterhouse entered both. Whilst Waterhouse was chosen for the Town Hall, Worthington was successful with his design for the courts. It was a very different affair from the Town Hall – the brief suggested a budget of £25,000 as against £250,000, and competitors were advised not to incur "any unnecessary expenditure in the external elevation." All the entries however exceeded the budget, Worthington's estimate being £35,700, and the final cost was £81,000. But this was modest compared to the million pounds spent on the Town Hall. The tight boundary of the site was also a constraint and it was with considerable ingenuity that Worthington fitted four courts together with all the ancillary accommodation into so small an area. The building rises sheer from the pavement, its massing designed to be seen in sidelong views and oblique glimpses down narrow streets (an effect somewhat changed by the recent demolition of surrounding warehouses). At one corner is a tall tower crowned with turrets and a steep pyramid roof. The style is Italian Gothic and the facades are characterised by groups of deeply recessed arched windows framed in stone and set in flat areas of orange brickwork. The rough masonry plinth, machicolated parapets and muscular tracery are suggestive of military architecture, and the fierce carved animals clinging to the sides of the doorways hint at the unknown terrors of judicial sentence. At the centre of the building is a tall chimney with an elaborate top, the visible expression of a technically sophisticated heating and ventilation system which Worthington had developed in his hospital and public baths projects. The courtroom interiors have been marred by modern suspended ceilings but enough of the original carved furniture and fittings survive to make an hour in the courts (as a spectator) a pleasant experience.

54

56. Manchester Law Library, Kennedy Street *(Thomas Hartas, 1885)*

In narrow Kennedy Street is an appealing group of small scale buildings which contrast with the grandiose piles erected on neighouring streets within the city's commercial area. There is the City Arms, a Georgian house with a Victorian pub front; an office building with plasterwork flowers and suns given human faces; and a brick block with bearded heads carved on the keystones. Most interesting is the Law Library erected in 1885 to the design of Manchester architect Thomas Hartas. It has large windows deeply set in a stone facade of busily traceried Gothic stonework. The abrupt termination of the front is the consequence of altering the design to satisfy the owners of Massey Chambers on the opposite side of Kennedy Street who complained about loss of 'ancient lights'. The original design had a taller and more varied skyline in stone. Hartas tried to achieve a similar effect by proposing instead an iron cresting with a central gable surmounted by the scales of justice, but the Law Society rejected it on grounds of expense and so the flat cornice was the result. On the first floor is a cosy reading room lined with dark oak bookcases heavy with legal tomes. Above the plate glass windows of the reading bays overlooking the street are stained glass panels by S. Evans of Birmingham, some depicting the stern heads of bewigged judges.

57. Thomas's Chop House and Hanover House, Cross Street
(1901; Robert Walker, and Horton and Bridgford, 1875)

In Cross Street is one of those enjoyable juxtapositions of buildings that only the Victorians and Edwardians could devise. Cheek by jowl against the sombre dignity of Hanover House, with its richly carved stonework and tall rows of windows, is the upstart sliver of a building that is now Thomas's Chop House. The former was erected in 1875 for the Manchester Conservative Club, attempting to outdo the Reform Club at the top of King Street. On the lofty first floor a large dining room stretched the entire length of the Cross Street frontage whilst on the other side a library overlooked St Ann Street. Above were two top-lit billiard rooms, a smoke room and a private dining room. The adjacent building is dated 1901. It is extremely tall and slim, enriched with an exuberant display of terracotta ornament, bow windows and cusped panels, all surmounted by a gable with a tiny pediment set on the top. Standing together side by side these two buildings are an irresistible reminder of Landseer's famous painting 'Dignity and Impudence'.

58. Barton Arcade, Deansgate *(Corbett, Raby and Sawyer, 1871)*
A ponderous facade on Deansgate conceals the only remaining Victorian shopping arcade in Manchester. There were others – such as the Deansgate Arcade across the road, destroyed by the blitz, and the Lancaster Arcade near Victoria Station, disgracefully demolished in the 1970s – but the Barton Arcade was always the finest. Its slender ironwork and curved balconies make delicate patterns against the sky, and light floods in through the lacy domes to lift the spirits on even the greyest of Manchester days. The iron structure came from Macfarlane's Saracen foundry in Glasgow and was assembled on site, but such materials were not thought proper for a major street frontage, so the Deansgate elevation is clad in stone.

59. Barton Building, 62-66 Deansgate *(Corbett, Son and Brooks, about 1875)*
Deansgate is one of Manchester's oldest streets, linking the site of the Roman fort at Castlefield with the settlement built where the Cathedral now stands. Its buildings postdate 1869, the year when the street was widened and straightened. The best section was from the Cathedral to Market Street where monumental hotel and office blocks faced one another across the busy road. But these buildings were demolished after bomb damage to be replaced in the 1970s with the ugly Market Place development. The next stretch too has been largely redeveloped but within it is the Barton Arcade and opposite that is Barton Building, a heavy stone office block housing Hayward's glass and china shop. The powerful rhythm of arched windows, different on each floor, is enlivened by a little frivolous carving, a contrast described by C. H. Reilly as "rather as if a frock-coated mourner at a funeral displayed every now and then a lace handkerchief."

60. Wholesale Fish Market, High Street *(Speakman, Son and Hickson, 1873)*
In the 19th century the area around Shudehill was busy with markets. Largest of these was Smithfield, first opened in 1822, where almost anything could be procured. The most interesting of the market buildings was erected by the Corporation for the sale of fish and poultry and opened in 1873. It was a glass roofed hall with basement storage. The cellars were entered through iron trap doors in the stone floor and each had a block and tackle for lowering and raising the boxes of fish. Off several cellars were ice-houses. Raised up on stilts within the hall were curious wood and glass pavilions in which the fish merchants' clerks sat at desks recording the day's sales. The great feature of the building is the series of six bold relief carvings in stone set in large arched panels over the entrances. They were carved by Bonehill of Manchester and show scenes of fishermen putting out to sea and returning with the catch. The two brick end walls with these carvings are now all that remain, for the fish market has moved out to Gorton and the roof has been taken away.

61. Air and Space Museum, Liverpool Road *(Mangnall and Littlewood, 1876)*
This fine exhibition hall and the similar structure a little further up Liverpool Road were built as the Lower and Upper Campfield Markets. The area was the site of both a popular open air market and the annual Knott Mill Fair which attracted visitors from neighbouring towns as well as Mancunians and Salfordians. The market halls were built to either side of St Matthew's Church, a Commissioners' church of 1825 which was designed by Charles Barry. Mangnall and Littlewood won the commission in competition with two other local practices, Barker and Ellis, and Corson and Aitken. Their design uses a structure of cast iron with an elliptical roof constructed of wrought iron and glass. It was used for many years as the City Exhibition Hall and has recently been converted into a gallery for the display of aircraft and space travel, part of the Museum of Science and Industry nearby.

62. Hyde's Anvil Brewery, Moss Lane West, Moss Side *(1861)*
Hyde's Brewery was established in Audenshaw in the early 1860s, moving several times before finding a permanent home at the Queen's Brewery, Moss Side, in 1899. The Queen's Brewery had been built by Greatorex Brothers in 1861 but was taken over in 1898 by the Empress Brewery Company of Old Trafford who had no need of the premises. The buildings are grouped around a cobbled courtyard, presided over by the brewery clock.

61

63 and 64. Chesters Brewery, Cook Street, Salford *(1898)*
The history of Chesters dates back to 1842 when Samuel Collins and Thomas Chesters began brewing at the Victoria Brewery in Ancoats. Threlfalls, with which Chesters merged in 1961, started in Liverpool but expanded into Salford by acquiring the Greengate Brewery in 1841. They added the Cook Street Brewery to their operations in 1861, abandoning the Greengate premises four years later. The present Cook Street building dates from 1898 when the brewery was greatly enlarged. Originally hemmed in between the railway, the gas works and the ironworks, the structure rises high over Salford to provide an

eyecatching skyline of tower and campanile. Seen above is the complex timber roof and lantern of the tower block; the Copper House is illustrated opposite. In 1967 the Threlfall Chester company became a part of Whitbreads and its identity was lost, but in response to the 'real ale' campaign, local names were revived and Chesters was once again adopted. Brewing at Cook Street ceased in 1988 and the building is now mostly vacant. An imaginative conversion is needed to ensure the survival of the only brewery left in Salford.

65

67. Lamb Hotel, Regent Road, Eccles *(1906)*

Edwardian pubs epitomise the architecture of display. Invariably occupying corner sites, they were designed to be noticeable by their ornamental gables and cupolas, oriel windows and shiny patterned brickwork. Flaring gas lamps illuminated them in the dark streets by night, their etched glass windows glowing with the warm light of a welcoming interior. The Lamb Hotel is just such a building, erected in 1906 for Joseph Holt's Brewery on the site of an earlier pub of the same name. There is a large full-height mahogany bar, glittering mirrrors, Art Nouveau tiles, and doors inset with thick glass, etched with the names of the rooms. In 1893 the landlord Frederick Greenwood lost his job and was fined the heavy sum of £100 for permitting gambling on the premises. But respectability had been regained by 1895 when the Lamb received a full licence, partly on the grounds that people visiting friends and relatives in the nearby Ladywell Sanatorium required strong revivers after their ordeal.

65. Plymouth Grove Hotel, Plymouth Grove *(1873)*

The fancy clock tower of the Plymouth Grove Hotel has long served its purpose of catching the eye of the passing traveller in need of sustenance and it is even more striking now that all around has been demolished. The hotel once stood in a prosperous middle class suburb but today only one of the large Victorian houses remains – 84 Plymouth Grove, where the novelist Elizabeth Gaskell lived from 1850 until her death in 1865.

66. Peveril of the Peak and Chepstow House, Chepstow Street *(about 1820 and 1900; and Speakman, Son and Hickson, 1874)*

The Peveril of the Peak is a jolly public house of the 1820s which gained its facing of multi-coloured glazed tiles around 1900. It has a good unspoiled interior of the later date with more tilework, panelling and splendid stained glass screens to the bar. Behind it, on the other side of Chepstow Street, is the multi-gabled facade of Chepstow House built in 1874 as a cotton warehouse for the buccaneering textile merchant Sam Mendel by Speakman, Son and Hickson. Mendel was one of the most notable figures on the Exchange. He dealt on an unprecedented scale, buying up futures contracts for months ahead and cornering whole sectors of the market. Through his warehouse passed a huge volume of cloth: "Night and day," commented his obituary, "a battery of hydraulic presses discharged volleys of bales for the East, and the West and the South." But the speculative nature of his trade did not survive the construction of the Suez Canal, and in 1875 the business was sold. So too was his palatial Italianate house in Whalley Range, whilst its contents, including a glittering art collection, were auctioned by Christies in a house sale lasting 21 days.

68. Victoria Theatre, Clowes Street, Salford *(Bertie Crewe, 1900)*

The Victoria Theatre was begun in style with the laying of the foundation stone by the great Shakespearean actor Sir Henry Irving in October 1899. It was Salford's third Victorian theatre and is the only one to survive today. The architect was Bertie Crewe, one of the most successful theatre designers of the day. In the late Victorian period, the introduction of steel allowed greater freedom for theatre interiors, and at the Victoria the galleries sweep round in wide arcs without intermediate support. Gallery fronts are decorated with rows of winged sprites and the upper boxes rest on muscular atlantes. But despite the jolly atmosphere and a programme of live theatre which changed weekly, the building was soon being used more for films than for drama. In 1919 it was converted exclusively to a cinema and thus it remained until 1958. After a period as a clothing store, it was reopened in 1973 as a bingo hall. Now the roar of the crowds is replaced by the rattling of fruit machines and the drone of the bingo caller.

69. Salford Cinema, Chapel Street, Salford *(1912)*

The Salford Cinema was opened in November 1912 under the ownership of Matthew Raymond who had already built the Arcadia Cinema in Blackfriars Road. It was a great success, praised by the *Salford Reporter* as "a credit and an ornament to Chapel Street" and "the handsomest picture palace in the Borough." It was certainly designed to make a show, with Baroque swags and garlands and an eyecatching corner dome lifted up on columns, all cast in orange terracotta. In 1913 a five piece orchestra was introduced and the films were shown to packed houses. The name of the cinema was changed in 1938 to the Rex and after the war slum clearance in central Salford affected its viability. The last film to be shown was 'Blue Murder at St Trinians' in 1958 and the building remained empty until 1967 when it re-opened as a Bingo hall. In 1985 it was taken over as the Victory Chapel. Where once mill workers surrendered their cares to the glamour of Hollywood dreams, the fervent message of the gospels now rings forth to proclaim a better life. The building is one of the country's best surviving Edwardian cinemas.

70. YMCA, Peter Street *(Woodhouse, Corbett and Dean, 1911)*

On opening in 1911 the YMCA building was heralded as a "City of Refuge from the Temptations of the City" and a "Stronghold for Jesus Christ." As a symbol of moral respectability it stands four-square, but it is a very elegant stronghold, its walls gently bowed and faced in subtly contrasting bands of buff and chocolate brown terracotta. The structure is reinforced concrete, the first important building to be so constructed in Manchester, and it was used to solve a difficult problem: how to accommodate a 60 x 20 feet swimming pool, a running track, a gymnasium and a 900 seat auditorium. The layout adopted had been pioneered at the New York YMCA. The pool, gymnasium and running track were placed on the top floor where they would secure the most fresh air and daylight and the hall went beneath unencumbered by columns. The main entrance from Peter Street is guarded by a copy of Donatello's St George, but the crusade for the minds and bodies of the youth of Manchester is soon to be transferred to new premises at Castlefield, and the Peter Street building has been sold.

71. Manchester Adult Deaf and Dumb Institute, Grosvenor Street *(John Lowe, 1878)*
This Institute was established in 1850 to provide education, recreation and religious instruction for the adult deaf and dumb of Manchester. It was originally based in rented accommodation in the city centre. In the 1870s funds were raised for a new building which was erected by voluntary subscription in the then fashionable environs of All Saints. It housed a large top-lit galleried meeting room, a reading room, recreation room and gymnasium, and cost £6,000 including land. The stone facade, in robust Gothic, would have contrasted with the plain Georgian terraces which formerly lined Grosvenor Street. Over the doorway is a carved shield showing an open hand placed on a book, the emblem of the deaf used in the 19th century. Above this is a sculpture of Christ the Good Shepherd in a canopied niche. The Institute closed in 1975 and the building has since been neglected.

Adjoining it is the Grosvenor Picture Palace, designed by Percy Hothersall and built in 1915. By this time All Saints had become an area of extraordinary diversity. At the centre of Grosvenor Square stood All Saints Church, and surrounding it were four other churches, Chorlton Town Hall, the Manchester College of Art, a Board School, a synagogue, the Chorlton Poor Law Offices, Righton's palatial drapery store, the Ear Hospital and various commercial premises. This was not as had been planned, for when the square was laid out at the end of the 18th century, it was to be the centre of an exclusive residential neighbourhood. Though some fashionable houses were built, the rapid encroachment of industry and workers' housing caused most of the select residents to move on. At the end of the century the population of Chorlton-on-Medlock exceeded 59,500 and the inhabitants were almost entirely working class. It was for this mass audience that the Picture Palace, with seating for 1,000 people, was created. Like most Edwardian cinemas, the building was faced in tiles. This was a material which was both cheap and showy, and at the Grosvenor, instead of the usual Manchester orange terracotta, tiles of contrasting green and cream were chosen. Since the war it has gone the way of most large cinemas – closure and conversion to bingo – but now it is a billiard hall, and whilst snooker has the eye of the television cameras, it may happily survive.

72. Church of St Luke, Cheetham Hill Road, Cheetham Hill *(T. W. Atkinson, 1839)*
Only the tower survives of what was the best early Gothic Revival church in Manchester. It was built in a prosperous area and the large churchyard was one of the most fashionable places to be buried. The style is Perpendicular Gothic, but the tower avoids the pasteboard character so common in churches of that period. Its architect, T. W. Atkinson, practised in Manchester for six years until 1842 but later settled in St Petersburg. The church was always a stronghold of Protestantism and in 1840 it achieved notoriety when the rector, Hugh Stowell, was accused of libel. He had stated that a poor Roman Catholic had been required by his priest to do penance by crawling on his hands and knees for four hours a day on the pavement in nearby Smedley Lane before the priest would administer him the Sacraments. The priest's action for libel was successful but the decision was overturned on appeal. Today the area is far from fashionable. The once elegant houses in Smedley Lane are ruinous and the churchyard is choked with weeds. But one of the church's prize possessions has been saved. It is a fine Roman Baroque painting of The Flight into Egypt by Alessandro Turchi which now hangs in the City Art Gallery in Mosley Street.

73. Church of the Holy Name of Jesus, Oxford Road *(J. A. Hansom, 1871)*
Manchester has no Roman Catholic Cathedral but the Holy Name is of cathedral-like proportions and splendour. It is the most important work of Joseph Aloysius Hansom, famous for the invention of the two-wheeled cab. The style of the church is 13th century French Gothic, its flying buttresses and rose windows reminiscent of Amiens or Bourges. Hansom's design had a 240 foot high tower and steeple, but only the lower part of the tower was built. The octagonal top section was added by Adrian Gilbert Scott in 1928. The interior is lofty and spacious with only the slenderest of columns dividing the aisles from the nave. From the clerestorey windows high above, shafts of light penetrate the gloom, and tiny candles flicker in the side chapels off the ambulatory. Externally the church is stone, but inside it is faced in creamy terracotta. The roof vaults are formed of hollow octagonal terracotta blocks to reduce the weight and so permit the immense span of the nave. The Holy Name was the first church built by the Jesuits in Manchester and was intended to seat 2,000 in comfort. Recently the parish has been disbanded and the future of the building is uncertain.

74. Church of St Mary, St Mary's Street, Hulme *(J. S. Crowther, 1858)*
St Mary's, Hulme, introduced to Manchester a new type of town church, noble, scholarly and intensely moving. It is the work of Joseph Stretch Crowther, first Manchester architect to adopt the principles of the Ecclesiological Society which aimed to revive in church building the spirit of the middle ages. The church is exceptionally tall, with a soaring steeple rising high above the surrounding tower blocks of Hulme. The lofty interior, dominated by the great east window, is simple and serene. Crowther also designed the ancillary buildings which crowd around the foot of the church. The rectory and school seen in the photograph were built at the same time as the church, and a second school beyond the rectory probably in the 1860s. In its picturesque composition and learned use of the Gothic style, this group was a model of the High Anglican ideal of a parish complex. For the church's patron, William Egerton of Tatton, it would have provided a symbol of spiritual hope in an area of unchecked industrial growth.

75. Church of St Francis, Gorton Lane, Gorton *(E. W. Pugin, 1872)*
The soaring profile of St Francis' rises like a heavenly vision over the drab wasteland of Gorton. When the area was built up with factories and orderly terraces of workers' houses the effect must have been no less dramatic, and so it was intended. For the church was built by Franciscan Friars as a showpiece for the Roman Catholic faith. The architect, setting aside the moralistic views of his more famous father, A. W. N. Pugin, on the need for archaeological accuracy, produced a building which is heedless of structural honesty. The west facade is given vertical emphasis by three huge mounting brick buttresses which support nothing, the central one sprouting out as a canopied crucifix. Above this is a thin bell turret and spire piercing upwards into the sky. The high chancel with its polygonal end contains an elaborate reredos, but the interior, despite its sense of spirituality, is disappointing, for the detail is mechanical and the walls lack their original painted decoration. Next to the church are the lodgings of the community, grim buildings of brick begun in 1864 and designed also by the younger Pugin.

76. Edgar Wood Centre, Daisy Bank Road, Rusholme *(Edgar Wood, 1903)*

Built as the First Church of Christ Scientist by the Manchester architect Edgar Wood, this is one of the most remarkable buildings of its date in Europe. It ranks with the work of Charles Rennie Mackintosh as an example of the avant-garde wing of the Arts and Crafts movement. Though Wood's primary source was the vernacular buildings of the north of England, he used their forms in a wildly distorted manner to achieve theatrical effect. Two features give the building immediate impact: the exaggeratedly steep gable on the main front of the church and the Y-shaped plan with diagonally projecting wings. Other elements – the circular staircase tower, the crucifix window, the tall chimney, the canted bay and the great round arched doorway – are then carefully grouped to achieve an abstract balance of forms. The building is largely of brick but the steep gable is emphasized by a facing of white painted render. The inside too is original. There is a simplicity about the plain white walls lit by dormers high up in the roof and the piers faced in green Norwegian marble. The timber organ screen has a latticework design like the grilles of an Arab house. Wood was chosen by the Christian Scientists for the artistic character of his designs and, unlike architects working for the established church, he was unconstrained by strict liturgical requirements. After sudden closure in 1971 the building was almost lost. Though some furniture was removed to the Whitworth Art Gallery, stained glass and internal fittings were destroyed. But after much procrastination it was finally acquired by the City Council and has been well restored as a centre for the performing arts.

77. Peacock Mausoleum, Brookfield Unitarian Church, Hyde Road, Gorton
(Thomas Worthington, 1890)

Richard Peacock was a self-made engineer, founder with Charles Beyer of the famous company Beyer and Peacock, manufacturers of steam locomotives for the world's railways. He was a member of the Cross Street Unitarian Chapel in central Manchester but, having established his home and business in Gorton, he determined to build there a new church for the Unitarian faith. His architect, Thomas Worthington, was a fellow member of the Cross Street congregation which included a number of influential figures in Manchester's public life. The Brookfield Church, completed in 1871, reflected the new spirit of Unitarianism which broke away from the austerity of the nonconformist preaching box and admitted the revived Gothic architecture of the established church. Thus the interior follows the Tractarian arrangement of nave, chancel and raised sanctuary, all adapted for Unitarian worship. The striking feature externally is the detached tower and spire, rising to 150 feet above the busy Hyde Road. When Peacock died in 1889, Worthington designed in his memory the mausoleum placed prominently outside the west door of the church. Below a Gothic shrine of white marble, raised on a tall granite plinth, the mortal remains of the great industrialist were laid to rest. At the four corners of the shrine are canopied figures: an engineer, a draughtsman, a blacksmith and, at the south west corner, the architect himself.

78 and 79. Church of St Augustine, Bolton Road, Pendlebury *(G. F. Bodley, 1874)*
St Augustine's is the greatest of the buildings erected by the philanthropic Heywood family; it is also one
of the most inspiring of all Victorian churches. The patron was Edward Stanley Heywood, a partner in
Heywood's Bank, and the architect was G. F. Bodley. It was built in a poor district, but Heywood's high
church leanings and advanced musical tastes were observed: sung Eucharist, Gregorian chant and
Gounod's Messe Solennelle set the tone of the liturgy. For the architectural setting Bodley transcended
Anglo-Catholic ideals of worship to create a pure and awe-inspiring atmosphere of spiritual beauty. The
church is set back from the road, rising like an ark from its bleak and desolate surroundings. Its towering

79

height is emphasized by blank expanses of brickwork and the tall windows placed far above eye-level. A tree-lined path leads through the churchyard from the gatehouse, passing a memorial to Heywood and Alfred Dewes, his brother-in-law and first vicar, fashioned in the form of a preaching cross. The path continues axially to the east end of the church which is dominated by a magnificent window with flowing tracery surrounded by a framework of blank panelling. The church was to have had a tower, a free-standing structure connected to the nave by a bridge with processional arches below. Only the projecting staircase turret on the south side indicates where it was to have stood. On the north side is the two storey vestry, a diminutive structure against the great walls of the church.

The interior is one vast space, the church roof high above, stretching unbroken from end to end. There are no piers or aisles; instead the walls are supported by internal buttresses pierced by narrow processional passages and connected high up by arches, a motif derived from Albi Cathedral. It is a space both solemn and austere – plain surfaces, stone floor, simplicity of carving. The eye is drawn to the glory of the east end, emblazoned in gilding and stencilling, and subtly lit by the pale colours of the chancel windows. The chancel is set off by Bodley's delicate oak screen, carved with fine tracery and surmounted by the base of a rood loft. This loft is incomplete, for it was intended to have an openwork front and support the rood figures of Christ Crucified, the Virgin and St John. The sanctuary is raised up by eight steps and dominated by a reredos painted by C. E. Kempe with tiers of saints and angels in the Sienese style. Bodley closely directed the design of the stained glass. The subjects are complex and include hundreds of figures: Old Testament kings and prophets, bishops and doctors of the church, orders of angels and archangels, and the apostles. The muted tones and restricted colours were selected by Bodley to create a more harmonious architectural effect and to accentuate the richness of decoration. Originally even the walls and roof of the nave were gloriously stencilled with foliage designs, motifs and inscriptions. The church has now lost its close-knit community of coal-miners and textile workers whose houses gathered round the churchyard. Its tiny congregation struggles with the maintenance of this vast building, appreciative of the beauty and importance of its charge.

80. Greek Church of the Annunciation, Bury New Road, Higher Broughton
(Clegg and Knowles, 1861)

The first Greek Church was established in Cheetham Hill Road in 1843 but as the number of Greek merchants increased it was decided to erect an impressive new building in Higher Broughton where most of the community lived. Clegg and Knowles, who were selected by competition, designed a severe classical church dominated by a tall Corinthian portico. The exterior is largely unaltered but the richly decorated interior was partly destroyed when the original barrel-shaped roof and supporting Corinthian columns were removed in 1962. There is still enough however to show what a sumptuous church it was. Within the polygonal apse at the east end survives the lavish 1911 decorative scheme by J. D. Crace of geometrical stencilling in red, gold and black, and marbled pilasters with gilded capitals. The fittings too are impressive: a great pulpit of 1919 exquisitely carved in marble and alabaster, and the superb wooden iconostasis of 1863 inset with panel paintings. The architectural splendour of the church testifies to the prosperity of the Greek community in 19th century Salford and still on Sundays the building resounds joyfully to the sacred chants of the Orthodox faith.

81. Manchester Jewish Museum, Cheetham Hill Road, Cheetham Hill
(Edward Salomons, 1874)

The mass immigration of poor Jews from Eastern Europe to the slums of North Manchester occurred between 1881 and 1914, but Jewish settlement in the city had already been a crucial element in its earlier 19th century development. The salubrious district around the Cheetham Hill Road was favoured by the growing community of Jewish shopkeepers and artisans and by 1871 there were over 1,400 Jews living in Strangeways and Cheetham Hill. The Great Synagogue and Reform Synagogue were erected close to one another on the Cheetham Hill Road in 1858, and in 1874 the Sephardi Jews opened the Spanish and Portuguese Synagogue seen above. The architect was Edward Salomons who was Jewish and lived in the neighbourhood. He based the design appropriately on the early Hispano-Moresque synagogues of Southern Spain, incorporating horseshoe arches, bands of different coloured materials and fretwork grilles. Inside there is gilding and patterned stained glass. But the Jews have deserted Cheetham Hill. The Reform and Great Synagogues have been demolished and the once thriving shops are derelict. The Spanish and Portuguese Synagogue has been saved only by converting it into a Museum of Manchester Jewry. It now stands, carefully restored, in a landscape of desolation.

82. Cheetham Town Hall, Cheetham Hill Road, Cheetham Hill *(T. Bird, 1868)*
Victorian civic functions at Cheetham Hill were of unusual splendour. Amongst the synagogues and Jewish shops stood a group of fine municipal buildings. The earliest is the Town Hall, a handsome Italianate design in brick and stone. Alongside is the former offices of the Prestwich Union, dated 1862, the headquarters of the North Manchester Poor Law Guardians. With its classical trimmings and fruity garlands it is decidedly ornate for a Poor Law Office. Beyond this however was the real showpiece, needlessly demolished in 1966. The Assembly Rooms, erected by Mills and Murgatroyd in 1857, boasted the most magnificent interior in the city, a triple domed ballroom fitted up by J. G. Crace in French 18th century style with relief carving, parquetry floors, gilding, mirrors and glittering crystal chandeliers. Now, the Assembly Rooms have gone, the Town Hall and the Union Offices have been abandoned, and the 'Land of Israel' has been taken over by second-hand car dealers and garish retail sheds.

83. Manchester Fire Station, Whitworth Street *(Woodhouse, Willoughby and Langham, 1906)*
The Whitworth Street Fire Station, occupying a large triangular block near Piccadilly Station, provided its occupants with a complete world. In addition to stabling, offices and storage for all the fire-fighting equipment, there was a laundry, gymnasium, billiard room, library and children's playroom, together with flats for 32 families and six single men. The men performed all the maintenance duties themselves: plumbing, painting, repairing the appliances, even an annual scrubbing down of the whole building for which crews were brought in from other stations. This kept the acres of orange terracotta facing in pristine condition and made the scantily clad ladies, cast by Burmantofts of Leeds, sparkle on the Fairfield Road facade.

84. Withington Hospital, Nell Lane, Withington *(Hayley, Son and Hall, 1850s)*
Like many medical institutions, Withington Hospital was built as a workhouse. For a use which caused such dread, the building is unwholesomely ostentatious, its architects using the Italianate style in a very debased manner. Facing the road is a stone chapel behind a gate screen flanked by lodges, and beyond this is the workhouse, a long brick range with sash windows and a deep cornice. On the far side is a building of greater historical importance, the workhouse hospital. It was added in 1866 by Thomas Worthington who took a particular interest in hospital design. In the 19th century hospital standards were lamentably low, particularly in the workhouses where there was often no segregation between the healthy and sick. This was one of the first hospitals in the country to be planned on the 'pavilion principle' promoted by Florence Nightingale, and takes the form of a row of five plain brick blocks, 100 feet apart, linked by a wide corridor. The layout was spacious in order to achieve maximum ventilation, and Worthington developed ingenious methods of changing and warming the air. The building is now hemmed in amongst the institutional clutter of a vast hospital complex but remains largely unaltered despite a century of progress in medical care.

83

85. Collier Street Baths, Greengate, Salford *(Thomas Worthington, 1856)*

Housing conditions in 19th century Manchester and Salford were notorious. Engels, who penetrated the Greengate area, wrote in 1844 of a chaos of one-roomed huts surrounded by a sea of refuse and mire. It was here that the city's earliest model housing scheme was built in 1870 by a public company promoted by the Mayor of Salford and the Bishop of Manchester. The designer of the scheme was Thomas Worthington whose commitment to social reform was unusual amongst Victorian architects. As architect to the Manchester and Salford Baths and Laundries Company he had already designed the public baths on the opposite side of the road in 1856. These were the first baths erected by this philanthropic company and they were an immediate success; nearly 3,500 people used the building during its first fortnight. The design, like most of Worthington's early buildings, is in the Italianate style, a robustly detailed two storey composition with a central attic containing the manager's flat. Originally there was a tall chimney in the form of a campanile, providing ventilation to the baths as well as a flue from the boilers. The model dwellings were demolished years ago and the baths look likely to suffer the same fate.

86 and 87. Victoria Square, Oldham Road *(Spalding and Cross, 1889)*

The chief object of 19th century housing reform was the improvement of sanitary conditions. In 1867, through the Manchester Improvement Act, the Corporation obtained powers to close unfit dwellings, but it did not provide alternative accommodation for their occupants. Combined with the demolition of slum properties for railways and commercial developments, these closures only increased overcrowding. It was not until 1889 that the City Council built its first housing, a tenement block in Ancoats. Designed by Henry Spalding and A. W. Cross of London, it is a huge five storey block with a central courtyard ringed by balconies. To modern eyes the effect is somewhat grim but in the 1880s Ancoats contained some of the worst slums, and Spalding had doubts about offering such hygienic dwellings to the working class residents of the area lest they should misuse them. For the facade to Oldham Road which might be seen by the wealthy passers-by travelling to their pleasant suburban homes, Spalding used good quality brickwork and introduced Flemish gables trimmed with terracotta ornament; at the sides where the inhabitants enter, the walls are plain. Yet the building, though altered internally, has served its purpose for 100 years, far outliving many of the more well-intentioned social housing experiments of recent times.

The dwellings within Victoria Square enjoyed good standards of light and ventilation; in the latter part of the 19th century this became a preoccupation of the Sanitary Movement. Bye-laws were established for new development, controlling street widths, sewerage, lighting and paving, and though at first these were disregarded, later they came to provide a formula for housing layouts with terraces in rigid lines, their backyards separated by narrow alleyways. An example of the Corporation's own model layout, Anita Street, seen in the photograph opposite, adjoins Victoria Square and was built shortly after it. Even the name Anita Street derives from the city's proud concern for sanitation.

86

88 and 89. Addison Terrace, Daisy Bank Road, Rusholme *(about 1847);*
and Marylands, Lower Park Road, Rusholme *(1860s)*

Victoria Park was opened in 1837 as a high class residential district to the south of the city. Initial plans were made by the architect Richard Lane who laid out large building plots and designed some of the early houses (at one of which, in Oxford Place, he himself resided). But in 1839 the development company failed and in 1845 the existing landowners decided to set up a trust so that work could continue. Toll-gates were built at the entrances and outsiders obliged to pay to drive within this select neighbourhood; at Park Crescent were handsome Grecian toll-houses and gate-piers. The earlier houses are stuccoed and classical, but most date from the 1850s and 60s and these are in a variety of styles. Addison Terrace was built in the 1840s as a speculation and in 1848 it was owned by William Broome Parker, a solicitor. It is a stucco terrace of 12 houses in the Tudor style, each with a pointed arched doorway and a door with delicate traceried panels. Marylands is Gothic, with steep roofs, tall chimneys and spiky iron finials on the gables. The walls are banded in polychrome brickwork and the facades are deliberately asymmetrical.

The park was the home of many eminent Victorians. Richard Cobden, the free trader and Liberal M.P.,

lived there. W. R. Callender, M.P. for Manchester, entertained Disraeli in a house on Conyngham Road. Sir Harry Smith, soldier, statesman and Governor of the Cape of Good Hope, lived in a large stucco house on Daisy Bank Road. Among residents of No 3 Addison Terrace, on the opposite side of Daisy Bank Road, are numbered two great artistic figures, Ford Madox Brown and Sir Charles Hallé, founder of the Hallé orchestra. Madox Brown and his wife leased it in 1884-6 whilst he was working on the mural decorations for Manchester Town Hall. Marylands was occupied in the 1870s by Edmund Potter, a successful calico printer and Liberal M.P. for Carlisle, and later by Sir Henry Roscoe, M.P. for South Manchester. It is now used by the Xaverian College together with the adjacent house which was built by Alfred Waterhouse in 1875 for the Hetherington family. The rich and fashionable started to desert Victoria Park at the end of the 19th century for the outer suburbs of Alderley Edge and Bowdon, but it remained undisturbed until 1920 when the Corporation obtained consent to run trams along Anson Road. The residents held out until 1938 before the toll-gates finally came down. When opened to through traffic, Anson Road was recorded as the second busiest route out of Manchester. Since the war there has been much demolition and decay, but 1987 was the 150th anniversary of the opening of the park and this event was celebrated with a hopeful determination to halt the decline.

90. The Shirley Institute, Wilmslow Road, Didsbury *(Thomas Worthington, 1871)*
During the 19th century a new type of house was established for the urban businessman on the fringes of the city. Called by *The British Architect* in 1874 "the country mansions of Manchester," they had the pretensions of the country estate but were close enough to the mills and counting houses of the city for daily commuting. The grandest of these mansions to survive is The Towers, built by Thomas Worthington for his old friend John Edward Taylor, proprietor and editor of the *Manchester Guardian*. As its name suggests, this is a house with a picturesque skyline: towers and turrets rise from the corners of the steep roofs and sharply pointed dormers bristle over the entrance front. Its style is 13th century Gothic but the outline is more reminiscent of the châteaux of the Loire. The massing too is varied and romantic; rooms are placed for convenience and aspect, their regularity broken up with projecting bays and recesses. The oak panelled interiors, lit by big plate glass mullioned windows, are heavy and serious. At one side is an Art Cabinet, a top lit room intended to house Taylor's art collection, some of which is now in the Whitworth Art Gallery. No sooner was the house completed in 1871 than the Taylor family moved to London, selling it to Daniel Adamson, a leading industrialist. At The Towers in 1882 Adamson hosted a meeting of wealthy Manchester businessmen and civic leaders, including 11 mayors of local municipalities, which led to the foundation of the Manchester Ship Canal Company. Since 1920 The Towers has been the home of the British Cotton Industry Research Association. It is named the Shirley Institute after the daughter of William Greenwood, M.P. for Stockport and a major benefactor.

91. Mynshull's House, Cateaton Street *(Ball and Elce, 1890)*

Mynshull's House is named after Thomas Mynshull, an apothecary from Cheshire who lived on this site, died in 1689 and was buried in the Cathedral churchyard. His will bequeathed the site to trustees for the apprenticeship of "poor, sound and healthy boys of Manchester in honest labour and employment." His old house was pulled down in 1890 and replaced by the fanciful Elizabethan style office building in red sandstone designed by Manchester architects Ball and Elce. A cartouche carved by J. Jarvis Millson records Mynshull's bequest. In 1900 remains of the old Hanging Bridge, a medieval structure which led to the Cathedral, were exposed to view by demolition of surrounding buildings, and 20,500 people paid to view them from Mynshull's House. Most were disappointed as the bridge, far from hanging, was largely underground. After much debate about preservation it was covered up again but today is partly visible at the back of the site. Britannic Buildings erected in 1906 makes an amusing neighbour. Just one narrow room deep, it rises five storeys with a row of half-timbered gables perched on top.

92. Peel Park Museum and Art Gallery, The Crescent, Salford *(Travis and Mangnall, 1852)*
Peel Park was the home of the country's first municipal free library and museum, opened in 1850. It was initially housed in Lark Hill House, a mansion of the 1790s erected by Col. James Ackers which had been purchased by voluntary subscription so that its grounds might be used as a public park. With the gifts of local families the museum collections grew and in 1852 the first of several extensions was begun by Travis and Mangnall which give the building its present appearance. It is a long block of red brick and stone with two handsome arched entrances, all in the Italian Renaissance style which was first used for museums at South Kensington. In 1851 Queen Victoria and Prince Albert came to the park where, gathered before them, 82,000 children sang 'God save the Queen'. Victoria described it in her diary as "the most original and striking spectacle ever presented to do honour to Royalty in any age." As a record of this visit the Victoria Arch was erected at the park entrance in 1859. It was an extraordinary piece of scenery, a triumphal arch designed by Thomas Groom Barker in the style of the Brighton Pavilion. The park was further adorned with statues of the Queen and Prince Albert by Matthew Noble and of local worthies such as Joseph Brotherton and Sir Robert Peel. In this century the park has been shamefully treated. The arch and Lark Hill House were demolished in 1938, the statues have been moved or sold, and the museum is overshadowed by an ugly tower block erected by Salford University. But the museum has shown foresight in one respect: it acquired paintings by L. S. Lowry long before he became fashionable, and this collection is now their greatest and most notable asset.

93. Brotherton Memorial, Weaste Cemetery, Salford *(Holmes and Walker, 1857)*

Joseph Brotherton was Salford's most important 19th century politician. He was M.P. for 25 years from 1832-57, a campaigner for radical causes, temperance, and most particularly the establishment of public libraries. Due to his efforts the country's first free library was opened at Peel Park, Salford, in the house where his Tory opponent, William Garnett, had lived. It was whilst passing the library in an omnibus on January 7, 1857, that Brotherton died. Only five days earlier he had inspected the new cemetery at Weaste and chosen his own burial place. The memorial appeal launched after his death raised over £2,500. £1,000 was given for a bronze statue of Brotherton by Matthew Noble to be placed in Peel Park, 500 guineas was invested to provide a purchase fund for the free library, and £1,000 was used for his memorial. A slender Gothic structure on an octagonal base, it was designed by Holmes and Walker, and carved by Thomas Williams of Manchester. A draped urn sits on the first stage under an open canopy, and above is a spire carved with shields containing the arms of Manchester, Salford and other local towns. Today the memorial has a forlorn look, no longer a place of pilgrimage for grateful Salford citizens. But it has been treated more kindly than the bronze statue. This was disposed of by Salford Corporation in the 1960s and was taken to the grounds of a country house in Cheshire. Recently it has returned, but to the wrong side of the Irwell. It now stands in Manchester looking across the river to Salford.

94

96

94 and 96. Salford Education Office, Chapel Street, Salford *(Woodhouse and Willoughby, 1895)*
Salford has no centre: its principal buildings are spread out along the north side of Chapel Street. As the
street is so choked with traffic, it is difficult to appreciate them, but one tall building which commands
attention is the Education Office of 1895. Until the 1870 Education Act, schooling had been largely in
the hands of the churches and the schools of each denomination tended to be in the styles chosen for
their church buildings. Since the new state schools were non-denominational, it was felt that they should
express a secular rather than ecclesiastical character. Generally this meant the Queen Anne style as at
Elliot House, Manchester's former Education Office, but the Salford Education Office is in the French
Renaissance style, its handsome facade entirely clad in shiny yellow terracotta.

95. Sharp Street Ragged School, Sharp Street *(founded in 1853)*
Manchester's first Ragged School was established in Sharp Street. Of the children admitted many were
homeless and a high proportion were orphaned or motherless. Though the school regime was harsh,
these formerly destitute children were fed, given a basic education and put to work in some industrial
occupation. The majority made a success of it and only a few returned to the twilight life of the streets.

97. GMBATU Training College, College Road, Whalley Range *(Irwin and Chester, 1843)*
The General and Municipal Boilermakers and Allied Trades Union enjoys the leafy grounds and ecclesiastical atmosphere of this imposing stone building in Whalley Range. It was erected in 1843 as the Lancashire Independent College with the purpose of preparing young men for the ministry of Congregational Churches. It is a surprising building for nonconformists, for at this date the Gothic Revival was associated with the established church or, worse still, with Roman Catholicism. Yet it is a serious essay in the late Gothic style, with a long ground floor arcade of Tudor arches, big mullioned windows and a castellated parapet. At the centre is a tall tower with clusters of pinnacles surmounted by a note of daring, an octagonal upper stage reminiscent of Fonthill. Beyond the entrance is an assembly hall added in the 1870s and in the wings to each side are classrooms and bedrooms. The college stands in fine grounds reached by a Gothic arched gateway.

98. St Bede's College, Alexandra Road South, Whalley Range
(Archibald, Dunn and Hansom, 1880)
Whalley Range contains a number of theological colleges and schools. For the Roman Catholics there is St Bede's College, founded by Dr Vaughan, Bishop of Salford, to equip the sons of gentlemen for success in business and professional life. The site was formerly occupied by the Manchester Aquarium which Dr Vaughan acquired and incorporated into the college. To mask the old buildings, a new frontage was erected in the style of the Italian Renaissance. Only eleven of the intended nineteen bays were built but it is still an impressive facade, tall and majestic in glowing red brick with much terracotta ornament. The grand entrance porch has large terracotta bees crawling over its surface and the doorcase is flanked by vivid blue ceramic columns. To each side of these are coloured plaques by Doulton of Lambeth depicting the arts, commerce, the law and the church. Out of the pediments of the ground floor windows the heads of worthies and dignitaries peer uncertainly like figures in a fairground booth.

99. Ellen Wilkinson School (former Nicholls' Hospital), Hyde Road, Ardwick
(Thomas Worthington, 1880)
Alderman Benjamin Nicholls was a wealthy businessman who used his position to encourage social reform. When his only son John died in 1859 after a brief life helping the poor of Ancoats and Ardwick, he set up as a memorial an educational institution modelled on Chetham's Hospital to take honest but needy boys from the locality. Worthington, who had been a schoolmate of the deceased son, was asked to design the building. Similar in style to the City Police Courts, it has a dominant central tower with angle turrets and a steep roof. A row of pointed windows marks the position of the original attic dormitories. Now part of the Ellen Wilkinson High School, the building stands as a powerful symbol of the Victorian ideal of charity.

98

99

100 and 101. University of Manchester, Oxford Road *(Alfred Waterhouse, 1870-98)*
The University began in 1851 as Owen's College, set up under the will of John Owen, a merchant of nearby Nelson Street. At first it occupied the former house of Richard Cobden in Quay Street, but in 1869 Alfred Waterhouse was appointed architect for new buildings in Chorlton-on-Medlock. Though Waterhouse exhibited plans for a quadrangular block in 1870, the scheme was erected piecemeal and the result is somewhat different. First came the low west range, then in 1883-7 the main east range along Oxford Road. By this time the college had become the Victoria University and as a new university it was felt necessary to make a show. This Waterhouse did by including a great tower crowned by a steep pyramid roof. To the right of the tower is the Museum, built to house the collection acquired from the Manchester Natural History Society, and on the left is the Whitworth Hall completed by Paul Waterhouse in 1902. On the south side of the quadrangle is the Christie Library, one of the last buildings to be designed by Waterhouse, and funded by R. C. Christie, Professor of History. These buildings make up the only coherent part of the huge campus which is otherwise a depressing catalogue of 20th century planning and design. Over the years virtually all trace has been erased of the unified Georgian terraces which formerly lined the streets of Chorlton-on-Medlock.

102. Grosvenor Building, Manchester School of Art, Cavendish Street
    (George Tunstall Redmayne, 1881)

101

103

104

103-107. John Rylands Library, Deansgate *(Basil Champneys, 1899)*
John Rylands, England's leading cotton trader, was a bibliophile and a devout Christian who devoted his latter years to philanthropic work and promoting evangelical education. When he died in 1888 his third wife Enriqueta determined to build a large theological library in his memory. To design it she commissioned Basil Champneys, architect of Mansfield College, Oxford, the new Congregational foundation supported by Rylands and other wealthy northern nonconformists. The building was to house Rylands' collection of theological books but funds were also provided for purchases and two major aristocratic libraries joined the Rylands books. The important Spencer collection of manuscripts and early printed books was acquired in 1892 and nine years later the Crawford library was purchased. Champneys was still a Gothicist long after the style had fallen out of fashion but at the Rylands Library he chose the Gothic style for its monumental and dramatic qualities. The church-like appearance of the building is deliberate, and for Champneys it was expressive of the old link between monasticism and scholarship. Only materials and workmanship of the highest quality were admitted: stonework inside

and out carved in razor-sharp detail, bronze entrance gates fashioned in Art Nouveau patterns, oak panelling, statuary and stained glass. No expense was spared in the realisation of this lavish monument, and the building alone cost £230,000.

Besides the main library, the building had to include a lending department, a conference room, refreshment room and a caretaker's house. To overcome the problem of daylighting on a narrow site between tall warehouses, Champneys placed the library on the first floor. The whole frontage of the building is given up for purely theatrical effect to a great entrance hall, and the progression from entrance to library is a thrilling experience with an unfolding sequence of vistas. The visitor enters the vestibule and passes through a forest of slim stone shafts before turning to mount a sumptuous vaulted staircase. Visible in the dim light at the foot is a large group statue by John Cassidy of 'Theology directing the labours of Science and Art'. The stairs are lit by tall Gothic windows and by an octagonal lantern above the half landing, from which shafts of light pierce the gloom. On the newel post is a luxuriant electrolier, one of the many original bronze fittings made by Singers of Frome. As the stairs are

mounted, the full height of the building is suddenly apprehended in the soaring space above the landing. The main library is no less impressive. It is a long space arranged like an Oxbridge college library with reading bays along each side and an upper gallery. The ceiling is vaulted and at each end are large windows filled with stained glass by C. E. Kempe. The reading bays are charming alcoves, each with an oriel window and separated one from another by traceried arcades. In Champneys' original design they were also to be divided from the central area by complex screens of tracery like chantry chapels. But as work progressed, Mrs Rylands became concerned at the overt religiosity of the building and insisted on toning down its ecclesiastical dress. This was understandable, for a library is a place for private study rather than religious emotion. Functional considerations however were of secondary importance to the aim of creating a fitting monument, and in the mysterious and uplifting interiors the scholar is transported far from the workaday streets of Manchester to a purer world. Lest the beneficence of the patrons of this remarkable building should be forgotten, there stand at each end of the library life size statues by Cassidy of John Rylands and his resolute widow Enriqueta.

108. Memorial to Queen Victoria, Piccadilly *(E. Onslow Ford, 1901)*

Queen Victoria first visited Manchester in 1851. Though she came again in 1857 to the Manchester Art Treasures Exhibition, and in 1894 to open the Ship Canal, she felt little warmth for the city and caused great disappointment by refusing to attend the grand opening of the Town Hall. Yet loyalty was maintained, and when in 1897, the year of her Diamond Jubilee, it was decided to erect a permanent memorial to the Queen, the public contributed magnanimously. The site chosen was in front of the now demolished Royal Infirmary in Piccadilly and the London sculptor Edward Onslow Ford was commissioned to create a statue in bronze. It is a grandiloquent monument; the Queen is seated in full state regalia, her robes billowing about her, surveying her subjects with a benign but distant gaze. Her throne is a great Baroque framework of white limestone providing space in a niche at the rear for a bronze figure of motherhood. It was only after the Queen's death in 1901 that the statue was completed; the unveiling was performed by Field Marshal Lord Roberts on 10th October, 50 years to the day after her first visit to the city.

109. Salford House, Bloom Street, Salford *(1894)*

In the second half of the 19th century Salford was one of the unhealthiest places in Britain. The death rate was acutely high: half the children born in 1868 would die before their fifth birthday, and in the older parts of the town the figures were worse. Overcrowding, damp houses, poor medical care, pollution and contaminated water were the principal causes. Even by 1900, 80% of all deaths in Salford were of children under the age of five. In this time the city had expanded greatly, but little had been done to relieve the old overcrowded part. One of the first public attempts to ameliorate the problem of homelessness was the construction of the Model Lodging House in 1894. It is a gaunt-looking building of red brick with tall windows to admit maximum ventilation to the spartan interiors. Over the entrance is the Salford coat of arms with the motto 'Integrity and Industry', a hollow message to the homeless and unemployed for whom the hostel was erected. When today we are told to admire Victorian values, it is a salutary thought that this building is still needed to serve the same function for which it was put up 94 years ago.

Alphabetical Index of the Photographs